Structure and Properties of a Wilderness Travel Simulator

V. KERRY SMITH

JOHN V. KRUTILLA

Structure and Properties of a Wilderness Travel Simulator

An Application to the Spanish Peaks Area

**PUBLISHED FOR RESOURCES FOR THE FUTURE
BY THE JOHNS HOPKINS UNIVERSITY PRESS,
BALTIMORE AND LONDON**

This research was conducted under a Forest Service–Resources for the Future Cooperative Research Agreement. Robert C. Lucas and George H. Stankey of the U.S.
Forest Service Wilderness Research Project were the principal Forest Service personnel
involved in this cooperative undertaking.

Jacket photo courtesy of U.S. Forest Service.

RESOURCES FOR THE FUTURE, INC.
1755 Massachusetts Avenue, N.W., Washington, D.C. 20036

Resources for the Future is a nonprofit organization for research and education in the development, conservation, and use of natural resources and the improvement of the quality of the environment. It was established in 1952 with the cooperation of the Ford Foundation. Part of the work of Resources for the Future is carried out by its resident staff; part is supported by grants to universities and other nonprofit organizations. Unless otherwise stated, interpretations and conclusions in RFF publications are those of the authors; the organization takes responsibility for the selection of significant subjects for study, the competence of the researchers, and their freedom of inquiry.

This book is part of the natural environments research program directed by John Krutilla. V. Kerry Smith is professor of economics, State University of New York, Binghamton. The charts were drawn by Federal Graphics and the book was edited by Ruth Haas.

RFF editors: Herbert C. Morton, Joan R. Tron, Ruth B. Haas, Jo Hinkel

CONTENTS

LIST OF TABLES

Contents

ACKNOWLEDGMENTS

The research on which this monograph is based was stimulated by some ideas presented in George Stankey's "A Strategy for the Definition and Management of Wilderness Quality" and the conceptual model presented in a paper by Anthony Fisher and John Krutilla entitled, "Determination of Optimal Capacity of Resource-Based Recreation Facilities." The latter established the optimal intensity of use of a wilderness area as that at which the incremental benefit of an additional recreation party was just offset by the external effects, or congestion costs, it imposed on all other parties that it encountered. The obvious next step in an effort to develop operational means of determining optimal capacity of intended low-density recreation facilities was (1) to establish the empirical relation between the benefits enjoyed during a wilderness outing as a function, among other things, of the number of other parties encountered, and (2) a means of estimating the expected frequency of encounters as a function of the intensity of use of any wilderness area. The first of these tasks was undertaken by Charles Cicchetti and Kerry Smith as a companion effort while the second is the task of the research of which this monograph is a part.

Much of the original work in brainstorming the travel behavior simulator that would permit estimating the expected frequency of encounters as a function of use intensity was done during the summer of 1971 with Charles Cicchetti, Walter Hagen, John Krutilla, Kerry Smith, and Walter Spofford participating. The basic logic of the model was developed during numerous meetings and certainly Cicchetti and Spofford are owed a special debt of gratitude for their contribution to the simulator's development.

The problem of programming the model for computer application was soon discovered to exceed our in-house capabilities and through the kindness of Emanuel Piore, we were introduced to David B. Webster of IBM, who, with Norman A. Heck's assistance, contributed the imaginative, incisive thinking required to convert the logic of the simulator into an operational computer program. Norman Heck's painstaking programming and attention to detail in the extensive documentation of the program

(Wilderness Travel Simulation Model, User's Manual) deserves grateful acknowledgment.

Data on user characteristics of the Spanish Peaks Wilderness Area used in this prototype application were obtained from surveys conducted by Robert C. Lucas and George H. Stankey of the Wilderness Research Project of the U.S. Forest Service, Forest Sciences Laboratory, Missoula, Montana. We are most grateful for their enthusiastic cooperation and willingness to assist with the use of their survey data. Moreover, early access to results of their research on wilderness users and their extensive first-hand knowledge of all aspects of wilderness recreation uses was an invaluable bank of background information which ensured that the simulator would incorporate elements of realism and relevance that would most assuredly have been omitted but for their contribution. Data required for modeling the trail system were assembled and processed with the assistance of Kerry Krutilla in exchange for the opportunity to participate in the field-checking of the trail network modeling effort, and desk calculations of transit times. The assistance of Lucas and Stankey in conducting the field work added greatly to the pleasure as well as the thoroughness of the undertaking.

We also most deeply appreciate the enormous amount of error-free, exacting work by Chris Sandberg in computing the frequency distribution involving user and trail system characteristics and in coding all of the processed data for computer input.

The computer centers at George Washington University and the State University of New York at Binghamton were most cooperative in enabling us to run the simulations reported on in this monograph. Mao Lin Yeh and Timothy Deyak assisted in coding the output of these runs for required further programs and analysis.

We wish to also thank Thomas Naylor and Walter Spofford for their careful reviews of the manuscript. Our other colleagues at Resources for the Future have also commented on the work at various stages. Most especially, thanks are due Blair Bower and Mordechai Shechter.

Rita Gromacki, Netti Rathje, and Sandra Soltis were indispensable in ensuring that eventually it all came out right.

While we owe much for the success of this effort to many individuals, we alone assume responsibility for any remaining shortcomings.

Resources for the Future   V. Kerry Smith
August 1975   John V. Krutilla

CHAPTER 1

CONCEPTUAL CONSIDERATIONS IN ALLOCATION OF WILDLANDS AND WILDERNESS RESOURCES

1.1 INTRODUCTION

Outdoor recreation has become a consumer activity of major economic significance in the past two decades. The demands for outdoor recreation engendered by the postwar gain in per capita income and the associated shifts in consumers' preferences have been truly phenomenal. So dramatic has been this development that even by the late 1950s perceptive students of the phenomenon referred to the impending scarcity of outdoor recreation facilities as a problem of crisis proportions (Clawson, 1959). During the mid-1950s the National Park Service launched its "Mission '66," a ten-year program intended to meet the burgeoning demands on national parks and recreation areas; the Forest Service undertook a similar program to develop forest recreation areas that were accessible by road; and many state and regional resource-based recreation areas were established over this period. But while some millions of acres of national parks, recreation areas, and state and local park facilities were added to the nation's recreational lands, many areas of remarkable scenic, ecological, or recreational value are still being subjected to increasing use intensity.

The growth in demand for roadless, remote-area, backcountry recreation has been even more rapid than that for easy-access forest recreation. Forest Service data on use of wilderness and otherwise undeveloped wildland areas, while less than fully adequate in many respects until recent years, nonetheless indicate a growth in the overall demand for such recreation of about 10 percent per year over the past three decades. Park Service experience with backcountry recreation in eastern national parks reveals a dramatic tripling of use in the six-year period since 1967, while the growth rate in float trips and camping on the Colorado River in the Grand Canyon has averaged 44 percent per year over the past twelve (1960–72) years!

In the case of wildland and river recreation, the problem of satisfying consumer preferences in an efficient manner, i.e., allocating available resources to their most highly valued uses, is a particularly challenging one. In special cases where there are no common property resources involved, and all of the costs and benefits are reflected in the prices of goods and services, the operation of competitive markets manages to allocate resources reasonably efficiently.

In the management of resources on the public lands, where the bulk of the outdoor recreation opportunities with which we shall be dealing occur, the problem is both more complex and more difficult. By law and public policy, access to some of the resources located on public lands is open to the public; i.e., they are open-access or common property resources, the services of which are not traded on established markets. Similarly, wild-lands and rivers, and even scenic areas, may be suitable for alternative and incompatible economic activities, with some uses having irreversible effects. Applicable law and public policy often do not provide criteria for disposing of incompatible claims that have adverse third-party side effects, including intergenerational implications.

For example, under the Wilderness Act of 1964, all unroaded areas in tracts exceeding 5,000 acres, on land under the jurisdiction of the resource management agencies of the Department of the Interior (except the Bureau of Land Management, pending passage of its organic act), must be evaluated for possible inclusion in the National Wilderness Preservation System. While not expressly directed to do so in the 1964 Act, the Forest Service also is confronting the problem of deciding on the allocation of unroaded areas—whether they should be recreational additions to the Wilderness System or reserved for forestry, mining, or other possible extractive purposes. If these agencies are to respond positively to the objectives of public land management suggested by the Public Land Law Review Commission, namely, to manage the public land so as to maximize the public benefit, they must compare the value of the service flow from each of the alternative uses to which the land may be devoted.

The same problem may exist even where the range of choice among alternative uses is restricted by law or policy. For example, while alternative extractive uses are not permitted on roadless areas (or elsewhere) in national parks, the question still remains as to whether the unroaded portion of the park in question should be added to the National Wilderness Preservation System, or used for more developed, higher density recreation purposes. In either case it is necessary to compare the benefits to be derived from a given use with those from competing alternative uses. The use of the resources for one purpose may preclude their use for other, incompatible purposes, and such benefits forgone are the opportunity costs of the selected use. These costs must be added, for benefit–cost comparisons, to any direct costs associated with the resources used in the chosen alternative.

Generally speaking, traditional benefit–cost analysis, in conjunction with inputs from resource management disciplines, can provide reasonably good estimates of benefits and costs of extractive industries operating with given resources at given locations. The art of estimating the demand for, and value of, resource-based, nonpriced, outdoor recreation services has developed in a most promising way during the past decade or so (Clawson and Knetsch, 1966; Burton and Fulcher, 1967; Cicchetti, Fisher, and Smith, 1973; Smith, 1975).

Perhaps less well developed is the methodology for evaluating the benefits from preserving irreplaceable natural areas, particularly those which are reserved for, or devoted to, low-density recreational uses (Krutilla *et al.*, 1972; Fisher and Krutilla, 1972). One of the reasons for the difficulty in the latter case turns on the question of the optimal density for low-density recreation activity at any given site. Maximizing the public benefits from a particular tract of wildland devoted to providing low-density recreation services will require that an optimal density be defined. This is only another way of saying that an optimal recreation capacity needs to be determined, and this will involve not only the benefits a recreational party derives from use of an area, but also the costs it may inflict on other parties by its possible contribution to congestion. This study will explore several important aspects of this problem; a conceptual framework for addressing it is outlined in the next section.

1.2 THE MEANING AND DEFINITION OF RECREATIONAL CAPACITY

There are two concepts of recreational capacity that should be distinguished at the outset.[1] The first we refer to as the ecologist's "carrying capacity." This is basically a biological or physical relationship between a given resource stock and its maximum sustained yield, i.e., the maximum number of individuals of a species that can be supported by a given habitat under conditions of maximum stress.

The economist's conception of capacity is also usually given in a physical measure, but in terms of a product of constant quality. Accordingly, when we speak of a wilderness experience as the product or service sought, we recognize that solitude as well as primeval setting are dimensions of the quality of the service. With a sufficient amount of wilderness area available to meet the demand for services, it is conceivable that a constant quality of the wilderness experience can be realized with moderate increases in use. However, at some point an increase in the number of wilderness users will

---

[1] This section with some revision is based on the paper by Anthony C. Fisher and John V. Krutilla, "Determination of Optimal Capacity of Resource Based Recreation Facilities," *Natural Resources Journal,* vol. 12, July 1972.

involve trail and camp encounters impinging on the privacy and solitude sought. At this point one would anticipate an erosion of the quality of the recreation experience. Deterioration in quality as a result of the external effects of congestion may exceed the economists' permissible level for optimal intensity of use substantially before the ecologists' carrying capacity is reached. Conversely, for some areas supporting fragile ecosystems, the capacity constraint may need to be set considerably lower than the otherwise unconstrained optimum if the ecological integrity of the area is to be protected. It is important, then, to note the distinction between these concepts of capacity and to distinguish them in our treatment of the problem.

Following Stankey (1972), but using an economic rationale, we shall consider a low-density (hereafter referred to as a wilderness experience) recreation use, a differentiated product catering to a relatively specialized clientele or submarket. Stankey has employed a rationale based on an extra-market allocative device (political process) for selecting his "public," "clientele," or in our terms, the relevant "customer," given the particular product market we are investigating. We can, as does Stankey, assume that the wildland tract in question has been designated as a *de jure* wilderness area, and our interest could center on determining what intensity of use would maximize the value of the service flow.

On the other hand, we can select for analysis a given tract in order to determine whether its value as a wilderness recreation resource would exceed its value as a high-density recreational resource. Stated differently, we could determine its value as a source of resource commodities exploited in a manner that destroys its integrity as a natural area. In this case, we would establish the benefit of the tract when retained in its wild state by fixing the use intensity at a level that maximizes the value of the preservation alternative; this value would be compared with the opportunity returns forgone if the higher density development or the incompatible extractive alternatives are precluded.

Our analysis assumes a multimodal distribution of tastes in recreation pursuits. That is, we are taking it for granted that those who seek wilderness recreation and those who prefer easy-access recreational sites *tend* to cluster in mutually exclusive groups.[2] Accordingly, in this analysis we are concerned only with those individuals who actively seek a wilderness-type experience. From this point on we shall be addressing that segment of the outdoor recreation market represented by the wilderness experience seeker, for whom solitude is a desired objective, i.e., the satisfaction or

---

[2] That is, the backpacker in the wilderness, a solitude seeker, is unlikely to be found at high-density vacation facilities. But preferences for solitude may be held ephemerally for "contrast," so that a lone backpacker during a vacation may be a socializing square dance buff at other times as well.

benefit gained from the wilderness experience tends to be inversely related to the number of encounters he experiences with members of other parties during a wilderness outing (Stankey, 1972).

We need next to review the analytics of determining an optimal capacity for low-density recreational facilities. Let us consider a relatively homogeneous group of recreationists who wish to enjoy a wilderness outing. We assume that an increase in the probability of encountering other parties on a wilderness outing is attended by diminished benefit for all individuals involved. For simplicity, we also assume a uniform distribution of users temporally over the recreation season. A season in this context can be segmented into as many intervals as necessary to ensure a relatively homogeneous experience. We could distinguish between the summer backpacking season and the autumn hunting season, for example. There may be other even finer divisions.

With these assumptions, we present in figure 1.1 a rather special set of aggregate demand schedules for wilderness recreation at a given area. The horizontal axis measures use intensity of the area, represented by the number of recreation days (or recreationists) per unit of time. For example, we suggest that q_1 represents a density half as great as q_2 and one third as great as q_3. Corresponding to each level of use of this area will be an expected encounter rate. Hence the vertical supply schedules labeled $S_1, S_2, \ldots, S_{10}$ denote the quantity of differing quality (as measured by the expected encounter rate) low-density recreational services the area can provide. The vertical axis represents the price or willingness to pay per recreation day. As the use intensity moves in thresholds (which are assumed for diagrammatic convenience), we expect the willingness to pay to diminish, since the quality of the service flow provided by the area at use intensity q_3 is different from that at q_1. Thus for any intensity of use within the range of 0 to q_1, we consider the quality of the wilderness experience constant. This experience, being free of adverse congestion effects, represents the highest demand schedule D_1D_1'. The total benefits of the recreation service flow per unit time with capacity fixed at q_1 (and fully utilized) are represented by the area under the demand schedule D_1D_1', here $OP_1D_1'q_1$.

Admission of additional persons seeking wilderness experience would be attended by the addition of benefits enjoyed by them. But an increase in the density of recreationists would result in a deterioration of the quality of the experience compared with the experience at the lower encounter level. The relevant demand schedule might then be drawn as D_2D_2' for a service with a quality now fixed by the use intensity represented by $0q_2$. The lower demand curve for the changed quality of service represents the diminution of benefits per unit previously enjoyed by those who experienced the wilderness with no adverse congestion effects. Accordingly, the

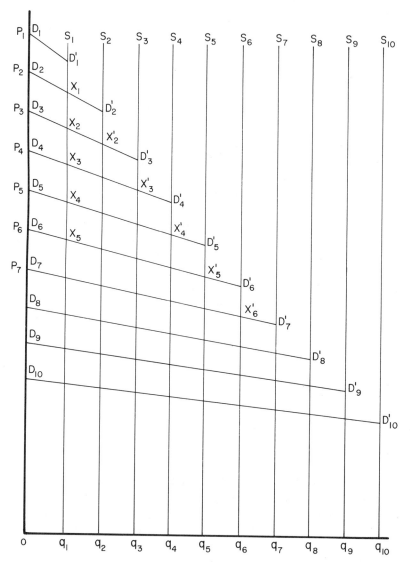

Figure 1.1

gain in benefits enjoyed by the additional persons participating would be represented by the area $q_1 X_1 D_2' q_2$. The loss is represented by the area $P_2 P_1 D_1' X_1$. As long as the gain from admitting additional persons exceeds the loss due to congestion costs, aggregate net benefits will increase. Beyond a point, the congestion costs exceed the gains experienced by the additional recreationists, and total net benefits diminish. In the diagram this occurs in the neighborhood of q_6.

Now, if there are no costs other than the so-called "externalities" or adverse effects of congestion, the maximum net total benefit level of use would also define the optimal recreation capacity for such a low-density recreation facility or natural area. But there may, and normally will, be other costs as well; for example, the cost of potential environmental degradation due to intensity of recreational use on some fragile ecosystem. Moreover, as Wagar (1964) and others (Clawson, 1968) have noted, costs in the form of operating expenditures may be incurred to reduce, modify, or eliminate the adverse effects of congestion. Furthermore, costs in the form of investment outlays to expand the intensive margins (e.g., laying out a duplicating but nonintersecting trail system to reduce or eliminate the probability of increased encounters with increased density) may, and in the normal situation would, qualify for consideration in a well-managed wilderness unit. Accordingly, the maximum total benefit as defined above is not likely to indicate the optimal recreation capacity for the wilderness tract in question. The reasons will be: (1) ecological degradation costs will not have been taken into account, and (2) the possibility of incurring expenditures in order to augment capacity must be considered at any time—and over time—in determining optimal recreation capacity for a given tract of land. To take account of these factors in our diagrammatic analysis, we need to return to figure 1.1, and from the basic notions contained therein, derive an additional set of geometric relationships.

If we now change our assumption of constant-quality recreation services within appreciable ranges limited by discrete threshold values, to an alternative assumption that these ranges can be made appropriately small, we can postulate a total net benefit function as shown in figure 1.2. Here we have the benefit measured along the vertical axis with the quantity of recreational services (user days) measured along the horizontal axis. All points on the total benefit function measured by the vertical distance when divided by the corresponding quantity will yield the average benefit, represented by the slopes of the cords shown in figure 1.2.

These average benefit computations can be represented in an average benefit curve such as B/q of figure 1.3, and the relation of the incremental (or marginal) benefit to the average and total is represented in standard textbook form as the dashed line in figure 1.3. We note in passing that the point of maximum net benefit (use intensity represented by q_6) is the point at which the cost of *incremental* congestion disutilities just equals the benefit of *incremental* gains to utility, and hence the *net* marginal or incremental benefit function at that point equals zero.

If there were to be no costs other than those associated with congestion, the optimal capacity would be given by the point at which the total benefit

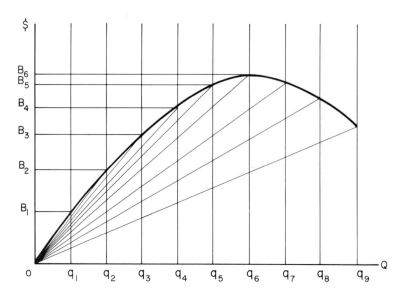

Figure 1.2

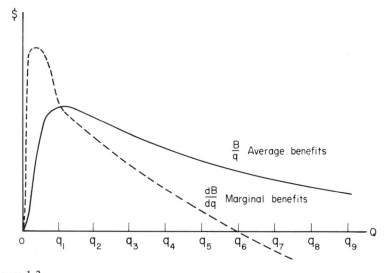

Figure 1.3

was a maximum and the incremental or marginal benefit was zero. With
the introduction of, say, ecological degradation costs, adjustment of the use
intensity to define the optimal capacity may be required. Conceivably one
could argue that the adverse impact on the area's environment would be
reflected in diminished utility to the wilderness user, and thus should be
incorporated, as were congestion disutilities, in the net marginal benefit

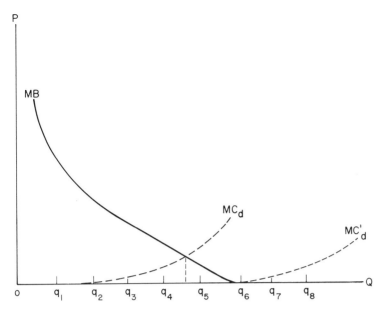

Figure 1.4

function. On the other hand, if such damage is extensive, permanent, endangers the existence of particular species, or in general will have a significant adverse irreversible effect on the ecology or more general wilderness environments, or both, it is likely to have disutility for individuals extending beyond those who may ultimately appear *in situ* to observe these effects directly.[3] Accordingly, it is desirable to show these costs in some way separate from the more conventional disutilities associated with congestion. We do so in figure 1.4 by means of a separate marginal cost of ecological damage function (MC_d) arising out of the adverse ecological impact of additional persons as the intensity of wilderness use increases. Now if such ecological damage were to take effect before the maximum total net benefit (excluding this latter consideration) was reached, we would show such marginal costs intersecting the net benefit schedule short of the q_6 intensity of use level. Thus ecological damage as the effective constraint or "limiting factor" would determine use optimally at a quantity represented by the intersection of a perpendicular dropped from the intersection of the MC_d

[3] The disutility here will include loss of an option to view an example of the remaining and diminishing untrammeled natural environment, whether or not the option will in fact ever be exercised. This option value will be of utility to an individual either for his own potential exercise of the option, or for its potential exercise by his heirs. For a discussion of this phenomenon, see Burton Weisbrod, "Collective Consumption Aspects of Individual Consumption Goods," *Quarterly Journal of Economics,* August 1964; Charles J. Cicchetti and A. Myrick Freeman III, "Consumer Surplus and Option Value in the Estimation of Benefits," *Quarterly Journal of Economics,* August 1971.

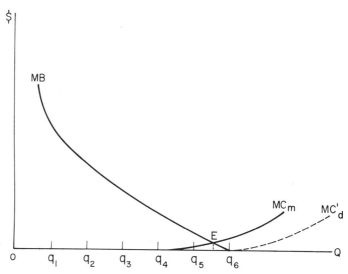

Figure 1.5

and *MB* functions, to the horizontal, i.e., in the neighborhood (just short of) q_5 in figure 1.4. On the other hand, were the maximum benefit capacity reached (where $\Delta B = \Delta C$) before the intensity of use resulted in non-negligible ecological damage, the ecologist's concept of carrying capacity would not serve as the effective constraint. This is represented by the curve MC_d'.

We need to attend to another practical consideration before proceeding to a consideration of capacity-augmenting expenditures. Up to now we have assumed implicitly that the costs of restricting entry to the wilderness tract in question were negligible. In a practical sense this is not likely to be true; thus some consideration of administrative costs is required for defining optimal capacity, other things remaining equal. In figure 1.5, assuming now that the ecological damage cost is negligible within the relevant range (between 0 and q_6), the net benefit will not be maximized at q_6, as when administrative costs were taken to be zero, but at some point short of q_6 given by the intersection of the marginal benefit function, net of congestion costs, and the marginal cost of administering the intensity of use (MC_m) indicated by the new efficiency point E, i.e., at a use intensity somewhat short of q_6.[4] The administrative cost here reflects simply an attempt to ration use, without affecting the spatial or temporal distribution of users.

---

[4] Since the services are provided independently of costs incurred for rationing, the equating of *MB* and MC_m is only a partial criterion. It is necessary also that the direct and opportunity costs of rationing do not exceed the reduction in congestion costs which they are intended to achieve. If the congestion cost reduction through rationing does not exceed the rationing costs, of course, no rationing is justified.

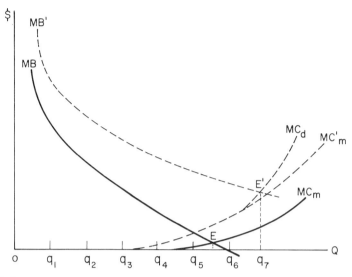

Figure 1.6

If we consider, in addition, the possibility of affecting the spatial distribution of use, for example, by redistributing users more uniformly over the wilderness tract,[5] we can consider more labor-intensive management to increase the capacity of a given facility without degrading the quality of experience. We show this in figure 1.6. Here the MC_m' curve represents the increase in management expenditures devoted to the more intensive management of the *recreationists* in order to provide a more congestion-free wilderness experience. The incremental cost shift from MC_m to MC_m' has the effect, as well, of shifting the marginal (net of congestion cost) benefit schedule from MB to MB', providing for all wilderness users a higher valued wilderness experience. This follows from the manner in which the MC_m' expenditures have shifted the (net of congestion cost) marginal benefit function MB'. This was achieved, by assumption, at an increase in both ecological damage costs (MC_d) for the increased level of use and of direct public agency management expenditures (MC_m'). We now have the optimal level shifting from a use intensity something short of q_6 to one in the neighborhood of q_7, i.e., below the intersection of the MB' and the vertical sum of the MC_m' and MC_d curves.

An alternative would be to reduce congestion costs by investment, e.g., additions to the trail system where topography and vegetation provide

---

[5] See Marion Clawson (1968), for an interesting discussion of the use of advance reservations, period of orientation, and dissemination of information to Boy Scout backpack groups at the Philmont Ranch, used to increase the aggregate number of recreation days without proportional deterioration of the wilderness experience.

screening, thus increasing capacity without a proportional increase in encounters or sightings. This would involve a tradeoff between more labor-
intensive (current) expenditures and capital outlays. It might also avoid
some disutility for a given amount of congestion by eliminating the element
of "regimentation" which regulating the time and place of wilderness use
would undoubtedly have for some. To show the effect of investment on
trails, however, it might be best to return to the form of the total benefit
curve (as in figure 1.2). We reproduce it in figure 1.7 as the *TB* curve
(compressed along the horizontal dimension). From any given initial

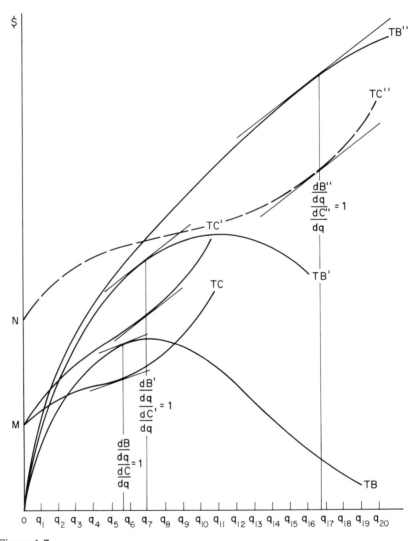

Figure 1.7

investment cost level OM (i.e., the present value of the opportunity returns forgone by precluding an alternative use of the tract), a total cost curve TC will trace both the fixed and variable costs, and the slope of the TC curve will give the marginal cost. The optimal capacity (at E, figure 1.5) would be shown on figure 1.7 where the slopes of the TB and TC curves were equal—where marginal benefits equal marginal costs—just short of q_6. The optimal capacity (at q_7) resulting from the shift in the total benefit curve TB to TB' due to additional expenditure on more intensive management (represented by the shift of TC to TC') is shown similarly, paralleling the exposition in figures 1.5 and 1.6. But, figure 1.7 can illustrate the additional effects of an investment, say, as an alternative to more labor-intensive expenditures to increase capacity.

Consider then an increase in investment of an amount corresponding to MN. Assume first that this is associated with an expanded but nonintersecting trail system which could accommodate larger numbers of individuals without increasing the probability of encounters. The increased capacity[6] is reflected by the change in the position of the total benefit curve from TB to TB''. The difference between the two benefit curves (TB to TB'') at any q represents the diminution of congestion costs due to the increased capacity of the trail system. To obtain the optimal intensity of use for the enlarged facility, we would trace the total cost curve TC'' beginning at q_0 from ON, and find the point at which the first derivative of the total cost curve TC'' equaled the first derivative of the total benefit curve, TB'', namely, where the marginal benefits and costs were equal. In the illustration using figure 1.7, this would be in the neighborhood of q_{17}.

Of course, to consider any level of investment as optimal, the level must be chosen so that the difference between the total benefit and total cost curves at the points at which their first derivatives are equal is at a maximum, i.e., at the optimal mix of current and capital expenditures. Moreover, if we are going to optimize, we will need to consider not only the relative gains between current and capital expenditures (operating maintenance expenditures versus capital improvements), but also the relative gains to capital outlays for augmenting capacity by *investment within a given wilderness tract* compared with *investment in additional wildlands*.

There is, however, an additional complication involving potential irreversible consequences when facing a choice to invest in the internal capacity-augmenting option as an alternative to adding existing *de facto* wilderness land to the system. If *de facto* wilderness, unprotected by legislation, is subject to depletion by other incompatible uses, the value of the present option will be lost, whereas the option to invest in internal improvements remains open. In fact, this option would remain as an alternative

---

[6] Defined as an increase in number of recreation days which can be accommodated for any given probability of encounter—or, alternatively, as a gain (reduction) in benefits (costs) for any given number of recreation days.

in the event the opportunity costs of holding wilderness tracts would rise sufficiently to counsel disinvesting in extensive tracts. Because these considerations are substantial, meriting separate investigation, we note them here only in passing. This treatment then, abstracts from the problem of defining criteria for choice involving irreversibilities and uncertainty. (See Fisher, Krutilla, and Cicchetti, 1972; Krutilla and Fisher, 1975; and Arrow and Fisher, 1974.)

We may summarize the optimality conditions (given the above qualifications) analytically by the following expressions:

(1) $$\pi = B - (C_d + C_m + C_k)$$

where π = net benefits
    B = benefits (net of congestion disutilities)
    C_d = cost of damage to ecological environment
    C_m = current expenditures
    C_k = capital expenditures, i.e., the relevant interest and amortization charges (or depreciation charges), the latter fixed by the relevant time horizon (or physical life of capital improvements)

Our criterion for optimal use of the area, maximization of π, is achieved by differentiating with respect to q, and setting equal to zero. Thus:

(2) $$\frac{d\pi}{dq} = \frac{dB}{dq} - \frac{dC_d}{dq} + \frac{dC_m}{dq} + \frac{dC_k}{dq} = 0, \quad \text{and} \quad \pi > 0$$

Or letting

$$MB = \frac{dB}{dq}, \text{ etc.}$$

$$MB = MC_d + MC_m + MC_k$$

i.e., the marginal benefits from an increase in recreational services (MB), whether quantity, quality, or the combination, must equal the sum of the marginal costs, whether they are in the form of increased management expenditures (current costs), damage to the ecological environment, or investment in extending the trail system (capital costs). These are generally all well-understood considerations in benefit–cost analysis. The problem, as in the case of all things which are rather well understood in principle, is application in practice.

1.3   SUMMARY AND STUDY PLAN

The definition and determination of "carrying capacity" of outdoor recreational resources was demonstrated to be a necessary condition for managing such resources to maximum advantage. Two independent sources of constraints on use intensity were noted. Where fragile ecosystems are associated with natural environments supporting outdoor recreation, the intensity of use, particularly for higher intensity recreation activities, may need to be limited by ecological considerations. This is the situation one may frequently encounter in the national parks where concessionaires' developed complexes draw large crowds, with adverse effects for the ecology. In the case of low-density recreation in wildlands, however, except for special circumstances, it is likely that the constraint on the intensity of use will arise from the adverse side effects wilderness users have on other wilderness users, i.e., the congestion externalities. The exception may occur when horse parties are drawn to particular locations because of the pasture that alpine meadows afford. The resulting overuse may damage the meadow ecology. But more typically, limits may have to be set on trail use because hikers or backpackers react adversely to encounters with other parties when they are seeking solitude and wildness.

This study will bypass an inquiry into ecological constraints or carrying capacity. It is not that these are unimportant, but rather that they are likely to fall outside the scope of this investigation, and certainly outside the technical expertise of the authors. This does not preclude independent investigation of ecological carrying capacity of outdoor recreation resources by others for complementary use with results of this inquiry. We concentrate, however, on congestion externalities in low-density outdoor recreation activities. This is an area in which important work has been done recently by behavioral scientists (Lucas and Stankey) in the U.S. Forest Service's wilderness research project. This work provides a foundation for our approach to the determination of optimal recreation capacity.

To do this, we need to obtain empirical estimates of the differences it makes in the benefits received by wilderness users if they are required to suffer intrusions upon privacy and shared experience of remoteness and seclusion during a wilderness outing. This must be done by independent research and econometric analysis that relates the benefits, or revealed willingness to pay for an outing, to the expected frequency and conditions of encountering other parties in the wilderness. This part of the problem was investigated in an earlier study (Cicchetti and Smith, 1973) and is briefly summarized in chapter 4.

In addition to the functional relations between the benefits of a wilderness outing and the expected frequency and conditions of encounter, we need to be able to estimate the expected frequency of encounters as a function of the number of parties, or intensity and character of use of the wilderness area in question. Since there are random as well as deterministic elements in the travel behavior of wilderness users, and thus in the pattern and flow of traffic, it is difficult to conceive of conducting experiments with actual parties a sufficient number of times within any feasible time frame in order to estimate the expected encounters with suitable variance at any given level of use. Moreover, similar experiments would need to be conducted at a sufficient number of different use levels to specify a relationship between these encounter variables and the use intensity, which is necessary for the determination of the optimal capacity or the point of maximum net benefits from low-density recreation uses. Since real world experiments with actual parties are not a feasible solution to our problem, we must seek an analogue to substitute for experiments with actual parties. This we attempt to do by developing a travel behavior simulator that is intended to mimic the behavior of wilderness users. It is described in chapter 2. With the simulator, experiments can be performed on the computer to provide estimates of the expected frequency of encounters as a function of intensity and character of use.

In chapter 3 we describe the data set and input data preparation for the Spanish Peaks Wilderness Area, our prototype wilderness area. Chapters 4 and 5 report the results of the experiments performed using these data with our simulator and test for the sensitivity of our conclusions to the quality of data, or the assumptions that were made in the absence of specific research data on the value of some variables. In chapter 6 we discuss how benefit functions estimated for users of this area can be used in conjunction with the results of the expected frequency of encounters at different intensities and under the different conditions of use postulated. We conclude with observations on the areas of further application and research using the travel behavior simulation model in chapter 7.

REFERENCES

Arrow, K. J., and A. C. Fisher. 1974. "Environmental Preservation, Uncertainty, and Irreversibility," *Quarterly Journal of Economics* (May).

Burton, T. L., and M. N. Fulcher. 1967. "Measurement of Recreation Benefits: A Survey," *The Journal of Economic Studies.*

Cicchetti, C. J., A. C. Fisher, and V. K. Smith. 1973. "Economic Models and Planning Outdoor Recreation," *Operations Research* (September/October).

————, and V. K. Smith. 1973. "Congestion, Quality Deterioration and Optimal Use: Wilderness Recreation in the Spanish Peaks Primitive Area," *Social Science Research,* vol. 2 (March).

Clawson, Marion. 1959. "The Crisis in Outdoor Recreation," *American Forests* (March/April).

———. 1968. "Philmont Scout Ranch: An Intensively Managed Wilderness," *American Forests* (May).

———, and J. L. Knetsch. 1966. *Economics of Outdoor Recreation* (Baltimore: Johns Hopkins University Press for Resources for the Future).

Fisher, A. C., and J. V. Krutilla. 1972. "Determination of Optimal Capacity of Resource Based Recreation Facilities," *Natural Resources Journal* (July).

———, ———, and C. J. Cicchetti. 1972. "The Economics of Environmental Preservation: A Theoretical and Empirical Analysis," *American Economic Review*, vol. 62 (September).

Krutilla, J. V., C. J. Cicchetti, A. M. Freeman III, and C. S. Russell. 1972. "Observations on the Economics of Irreplaceable Assets," in *Environmental Quality Analysis*, edited by A. V. Kneese and B. T. Bower (Baltimore: Johns Hopkins University Press for Resources for the Future).

———, and A. C. Fisher. 1975. *The Economics of Natural Environments: Studies in the Valuation of Commodity and Amenity Resources* (Baltimore: Johns Hopkins University Press for Resources for the Future).

One Third of the Nation's Land. 1970. A Report to the President and to the Congress by the Public Land Law Review Commission (Washington, D.C.).

Smith, V. K. 1975. "The Estimation and Use of Models of the Demand for Outdoor Recreation," paper prepared for the National Academy of Sciences in *Assessing the Demand for Outdoor Recreation* (Washington, D.C.: National Academy of Sciences).

Stankey, G. H. 1972. "A Strategy for the Definition and Management of Wilderness Quality," in *Natural Environments: Studies in Theoretical and Applied Analysis*, edited by J. V. Krutilla (Baltimore: Johns Hopkins University Press for Resources for the Future).

Wagar, J. A. 1964. *The Carrying Capacity of Wildlands for Recreation*, Forest Service Monograph 7.

CHAPTER 2

AN OUTLINE OF THE WILDERNESS TRAFFIC SIMULATOR

2.1 INTRODUCTION

This chapter briefly summarizes a large-scale traffic simulation model developed by Resources for the Future jointly with IBM. As we noted in the first chapter, the measurement of the effects of different use patterns on the quality of the experiences available in low-density recreational areas cannot be determined easily with real world experimentation and data collection. The record keeping and time lags involved suggested that some alternative methods for analyzing these problems had to be developed.

Consequently we have chosen to simulate the activities which occur in these areas and play out alternative scenarios with our model. Clearly the accuracy of our results depends on two factors: (1) the fidelity of our model in representing actual wilderness users' behavior patterns, i.e., how adequately it mimics the actions of wilderness users, and (2) the accuracy of the input data (to be described in chapter 3) developed for each area to be simulated.

Since there is an extensive user manual available for the program and this study is designed to serve a complementary function, our description will be brief and heuristic. After a general description of the model, sections of this chapter will address the scheduling of parties, the definition and assignment of routes, the recording of encounters, and the data collection functions of the program.

2.2 A GENERAL DESCRIPTION OF THE SIMULATION MODEL

In many respects, wilderness or low-density recreational activities are unique to each individual enthusiast and therefore they are unlike the conventional processes that are modeled using simulation analysis. Characteristically, it is not possible for individuals to enumerate an all-inclusive set of criteria for evaluating a wilderness trip. Different individuals will seek to realize perhaps somewhat different objectives from their trips.

However, as we have noted in chapter 1, considerable progress has been made in defining the relevant variables for judging the quality of wilderness recreation. Two developments contribute to this. First, the work of George Stankey (1971) has directed attention to the factors that should be reflected in managerial objectives.[1] Second, Stankey's research has suggested that the values shared by wilderness users are reflected in the 1964 Wilderness Act.[2] Moreover, further survey research by Cicchetti and Smith (1973) reinforces his findings.

In general, wilderness users seek a recreational experience remote from typical work-a-day activities, with a measure of seclusion as a primary attribute. One means of characterizing alternative wilderness experiences then is according to the solitude the individual user enjoys during a trip of given length. It is not obvious how solitude should be measured; however, Stankey's work suggests that encounters with individuals not of one's own party can be expected to yield a reasonably good index of intrusions on privacy and reduction of satisfaction. The further research of Cicchetti and Smith (1973) reinforces his findings and suggests that encounters (i.e., meetings between wilderness parties) classified by the modes of travel of the parties involved are significant determinants of the amount users are willing to pay for low-density recreation. The place of encounter, whether on the trail or in camp, is also an important characteristic of the intrusion upon solitude.

It is not unreasonable to suggest that the activity of wilderness recreation—in which many parties of various sizes and travel modes utilize a given area for different lengths of time—is not amenable to mathematical modeling. That is, mathematical representation of the behavioral patterns of users suffers from several shortcomings. (1) The inherent complexity of the behavior pattern would of necessity prevent differential equation models of individual movements from being useful. (2) The size (i.e., number of parties) of the user population at any time during a season as well as the complexity of most wilderness areas also precludes any mathematical description. (3) Finally, it is not clear that the relevant output variables for measuring system performance are subject to unambiguous definition in a simple mathematical structure.

Given these obstacles, simulation modeling provides the most realistic and tractable approach to the problem. The simulation approach calls for the design of a process which approximates as nearly as possible the actual activities of recreationists. That is, our model will attempt to replicate the travel behavior of wilderness users. In one sense it is analogous to the

---

[1] The economic rationale being that the public provision of recreational services ought to provide the same kind of diversity of experiences available for goods that exchange in well-organized markets.

[2] See Stankey (1972), pp. 112–114.

controlled experimentation of the natural sciences. Utilizing advanced computer technology, we can produce scenarios which simulate the activities of all recreationists in a given area. Once a simulator for this purpose is constructed and we have reason to believe it,[3] then we can monitor the activities and record that information which is important for managerial decision making. For example, we can record the number and types of encounters each party has during its trip in the area; or account can be kept of those segments in the trail system and the campsites which were most heavily used.

Once the aspects of the model which are important can be enumerated and the performance variables defined, the simulation model can be defined as an intricate scheduling problem. That is, we can think of any party of wilderness users as undergoing a sequence of processes before it can leave the area. Our model is concerned with the definition of a party's schedule, its execution, and the record keeping as the party progresses along its schedule. Parties move through a sequence of trail segments and campsites in a definite pattern which we shall assume is a function of their mode of travel and the length of their trip. Moreover, we must allow for variability in speeds by mode of travel, size of the party, segment they may be traversing, and a randomization factor. Changes in the grade or the general condition of the trail will affect these speeds. In our application of the model to the Spanish Peaks Wilderness Area, careful attention was given to the determination of these speeds and, therefore, to the time spent on any particular segment. Chapter 3 describes the process of estimating them.

There are four important steps in the simulation of wilderness travel behavior. Each of these will be discussed in detail in what follows. However, in order to provide perspective, we shall outline how they all fit together for the model as a whole. The first part of the model, logically preceding all else in the process, is the schedule of arrivals. Based on historical evidence,[4] it is reasonable to suggest that users arrive at a given area under some schedule. This does not mean that we are assuming the decisions of all recreational trips are made jointly, but rather that we can define an arrival schedule such as that given in figure 2.1. Note that this illustration defines the number of parties that come to a particular area in

---

[3] Validation of this simulation model based on actual data from the monitoring of wilderness use is difficult, if not impossible. We have relied on validation by a group of experts in the U.S. Forest Service and Resources for the Future. In their judgment, the logical process depicted by the model approximates reasonably well the real world activities.

[4] For our purposes a sample compiled by Robert Lucas and George Stankey of wilderness users in the Spanish Peaks Wilderness Area is the basis for our estimates of these arrival patterns. However, mandatory registration being instituted by the U.S. Forest Service is likely to make this kind of data more readily available.

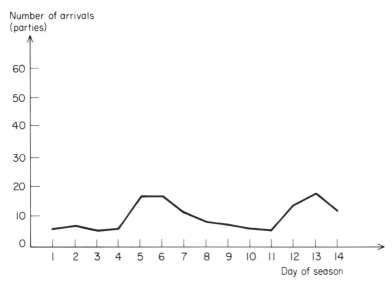

Figure 2.1

a two-week period. We would like our model to approximate as nearly as possible the pattern of arrivals to the area. Thus our simulation model must define a schedule similar to that given in figure 2.1. While it will need to be more specific than this graph implies, the essential idea is analogous. Once individual arrivals are scheduled, we want the mix of parties to be representative of actual experience—both in the size of the parties and in their mode of travel. Thus it is necessary to assign a set of characteristics to each party when it is scheduled, so that the characteristics can be used in further scheduling and can serve as parameters for identifying groups with the total set of all parties in a given area.

Once the schedule of arrivals is defined and characteristics are assigned to each arrival, it is necessary to define what each party will do once in the area. There are several ways in which this decision can be made. One would be to assign parties to points of entry and let their trips, once in the area, be arbitrarily determined, say through a sequence of probability functions at each possible decision point within the system. A second alternative is to designate a set of routes which would be assumed to describe all possible travel patterns or trips for a given area. Each party would be assigned one of these routes and further decisions would be predetermined by route plan. Finally, one might think of a scheme which calls for a mixture of these two approaches.[5]

---

[5] That is, one might think of a party making changes in its trip based on the extent to which it has had encounters with others in the initial parts of its route plan.

For a number of reasons, the second approach was selected as being the most realistic in terms of providing the ability to replicate observed behavior and in terms of the party's own decision making. Both the first and the last general approaches do not allow the model to replicate observed behavior. That is, we cannot *a priori* designate a traffic pattern which conforms with that observed in the real world. Rather, after the model has run we must compare the randomly defined routes with those actually selected. There are no guarantees that the correspondence will be reasonable. Moreover, the likelihood of "outlier behavior," that is, trips which cannot be considered representative under any definition, is much greater with either the first or last approaches.

Thus far these functions have addressed various parts of the initializing or definition of the composition of the users and implicitly the characteristics of the system (i.e., wilderness or primitive area) they will utilize. The execution of the model requires some control mechanism as well as an information base. For example, the reason why mode of travel is important is that it will affect the time it takes a party to traverse a given segment. This information must be available for each party type and size as well as for each trail segment in the area under study. The control mechanism is the "clock" that advances each party along its preassigned schedule, thereby moving the "traffic" through the area and simulating behavior. The clock is "event-driven" in that it advances time in discrete intervals, where the length of the time interval is determined by the minimum time for any party to change its status.[6]

Perhaps the most important single component of this simulation model is the mechanism for recording encounters. Past research has indicated that the place of encounter, whether it occurs on the trail or in camp, and the character of the party encountered (i.e., its size and mode of travel) will be important factors influencing the degree to which satisfaction with the wilderness trip is diminished for an individual. Consequently, the program must record these events according to these dimensions, if the model is to reflect how alternative management strategies will affect the quality of an individual's wilderness trip.

A final and not inconsequential component of the model is the mechanism for collecting and summarizing the information on the events which took place during the simulation. As the following discussion will illustrate, each simulation run is one replication of a stochastic process, in that many of the output variables are random. Consequently, attention must be given to the design of experiments which will provide information on the performance of alternative management strategies within tolerable error margins. Moreover, it is necessary to distinguish (1) the variation across

[6] See Naylor (1971) for a complete description of this approach to simulation.

parties of similar characteristics in a given simulation run of the model from (2) the variation between identically structured replications of the simulation model. Both sources of variation are important and their respective roles will be addressed in chapter 4.

2.3   THE SCHEDULING OF PARTIES

The process of scheduling parties for the simulation model is an attempt to construct a pattern of arrivals to the area being investigated which conforms to that observed in practice.

It does not mean that the model implicitly assumes the arrivals to a wilderness area correspond to an advance registration system nor any other formal system of rationing use. Rather, it is a mechanism for representing what actually happens at a given area or what managers think is likely to take place. In order to define this comprehensive schedule, it is necessary to make several decisions. The first of these is the length of time, in weeks, in which the simulation model will run. That is, what is the length of the season or fraction of a season in which we plan to examine the experiences of wilderness users? Given this decision, it is possible to define the total number of parties that will arrive in this period.

Our schedule then allocates these parties to each week in that defined period, within each week to the day of the week, and then within the day to each hour. This allocation process is important for several reasons. First, it determines the bunching of parties across the weeks and may thereby depict peak periods or distinguish weekend use from that of week-days. In terms of figure 2.1 the arrivals increase on days five, six, twelve, and thirteen—corresponding to the Fridays and Saturdays of the two weeks. Equally important, the schedule in the course of any day can affect the recorded number of meetings by bunching parties within certain hours of the day. Ideally, the decisions on these specifications should be data based. That is, if we wish to simulate real world existing conditions, the frequency distributions should be based on observed patterns of arrivals.

Another important aspect of the scheduling is our ability to replicate certain managerial options. That is, advance registration might be expected to smooth the distribution of use across the weeks of a season and perhaps even the days within a week. By comparing the results of a data-based schedule with those of smoothed distributions that can reasonably be assumed to follow as a result of a managerial action, we are, in effect, examining the implications of this policy.

In our model, certain stages of these allocation schemes are probabilistic and others are exact. To assure the entry of the prespecified number of parties in the time of the simulation, the allocation of parties to weeks within the season is exact. In terms of the specific programming language, one party is generated each week and it is "split"[7] or matched by a number of parties so that the total for each week corresponds to that fraction designated by the program user. Given this number, each party is scheduled to a day using one of three preassigned probability distributions. In each case a pseudorandom number from a uniform distribution on the interval from 0 to 1 is generated, and is compared with the appropriate cumulative probability distribution. Based on this comparison, the party is assigned to arrive on the corresponding day. For example, if approximately 25 percent of the parties arrive on Monday and 10 percent on Tuesday, then if the random number so generated falls between 0 and 25/100, the party is assigned to arrive on Monday. If it is between 25/100 and 35/100, the party is designated to arrive on Tuesday. If the value is greater than 35, then it is assigned to another day, depending on the remainder of the appropriate cumulative distribution.

In a similar fashion,[8] the parties are distributed across the hours of the day. Several important points should be noted before proceeding. The program allows the user to designate three daily distributions. That is, each week in the season can be defined, in terms of the arrivals of parties, according to one of three types of daily probability distributions. Hence in a single run the distinction can be made between early and late season user patterns, or between holiday weeks and those without holidays. In contrast, the distribution of parties across the hours of the day is the same for all days. While it can be respecified, the distribution must be assumed to hold for all days of the week.

The assignment of parties to various weeks in the simulation run is exact, but the distribution across the days of the week or the hours of any day can be assumed to vary as a result of their probabilistic character. On average, over a number of replications they will correspond to the assigned distributions.

These three operations define the exact time within the simulation run in which each party will enter the area. We do not as yet know the party's characteristics nor what it will do on entry. We have assumed that three factors will affect what a party will do on entering the area. Two of these relate to the scheduling of the party's entry. First, the time of arrival—morning or afternoon—will affect actions, since it is expected that parties entering in the afternoon will select routes that have campsites within

---

[7] The split block creates copies of the transaction entering the block with the entering transaction as parent. Since at this stage in the scheduling no characteristics have been assigned, all parties are alike. At a later point after the split, distinguishing characteristics are incorporated.

[8] There is, however, an important distinction. For the hourly distributions the cumulative functions are assumed to be piecewise continuous for the time intervals involved, so that parties are uniformly distributed within these intervals. The distributions across the days of the week are discrete-valued probability functions.

reasonable proximity to the entry point. This discretionary safeguard is designed to prevent the model from assigning route plans to parties which call for their travel until late hours in simulation time. Moreover, it allows added flexibility in the specification of the behavior patterns. The second characteristic of parties that is assumed to affect their routes or traveling pattern in the area is their mode of travel. We have allowed for differences between the selections of hiking versus riding parties. One need not specify differences, but if the data indicate differences, they can be accounted for. Moreover, if the planner wishes to examine the implications of segmenting an area so that certain users are restricted to portions of the facility, this conditioning factor is one convenient way of designing such a scenario.

The models assign the mode of travel according to preselected probability distributions. Three distributions can be specified and assigned to alternative weeks in the simulated time. That is, it is possible to change the distribution of riding parties from week to week, so long as the alternative mixes correspond to one of three preassigned probability distributions. This option requires yet another definition of week-type. In this case the week-type defines which probability distribution will be used to designate the mode of travel. Finally, each party is given a particular size. These specifications have been kept fairly general in that they define parties as small, medium, and large. Our reasoning here is to maintain flexibility. A small party for one area may not be small for another area. Thus the researcher can attach sizes to these ordinal classifications. The assignment of party size is also probabilistic, with the distribution conditioned on the party's mode of travel (i.e., hiking versus riding).

The size and mode of travel as well as a unique index identifying each party are informational parameters retained by the party until it leaves the system with its simulated trip complete. They will be important for recording types of encounters and therefore for evaluation of the quality of the experiences an area can provide its users under alternative use patterns and management strategies.

2.4 THE ASSIGNMENT OF ROUTES

As we noted, the assignment of the travel behavior of a party in the area being studied is established as a part of the definition and scheduling of the party. Once given, no variations on the pattern are allowed. In order to accomplish this, we must first define a set of trips or route plans for the set of all possible routes. That is, given any trail network, it is possible to define a very large number of ordered sequences through the network, and we must be able to screen patterns of use that are unreasonable from those that are reasonable. Once again we have assumed that empirical data on use patterns are the best means of defining the relevant

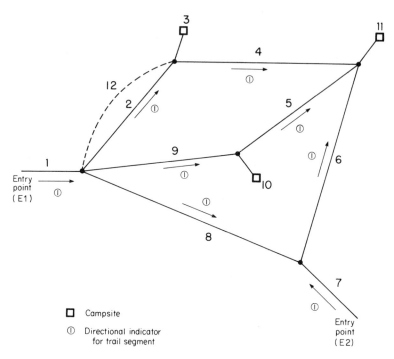

Figure 2.2

sample space of trips. Consider figure 2.2 as an example of a hypothetical wilderness area. The numbered segments represent trail segments while the numbered boxes designate campsites.

A route is defined as an ordered sequence of trail and camp segments. Examination of this figure indicates that not only must the trails be specified but also the direction on any one segment as well. Hence directional arrows are included in the figure, with a circled "1" indicating the one direction.[9]

These directional indicators are important for several reasons. First, the set of routes with the directions indicated is the only description of the trail network provided to the computer in the simulation. It must be consistent and correspond with the actual area if we are to believe our output measures. For example, one route might be defined as entering at 1, moving along segment 2 in the "one" direction and returning in the opposite direction to 1. We can also define a route that allows entry at 1 and moves along segment 2 toward 1 as the next step (i.e., opposite to the arrow); this is clearly impossible from the map. It is not, however, impossible from route

[9] In the coding of routes, these directional indicators are appended to the trail segment identification numbers.

definition. It is the responsibility of the researcher to ensure the logical consistency between the route definition and its feasibility in terms of the trail system.

A second important role for these directional indicators is in changing the transit times. That is, in order to reflect the effect of differences in trail gradients on transit time, we provide for differences in the time it takes a party to traverse a segment. Direction will be important to this effect. Going up a mildly rising grade will have a different effect upon the party's speed than descending along the same segment.

Thus a route defines the segments over which the party will travel. It specifies the direction traveled. Campsites are also included in the specifications and, therefore, by definition the length of trip is also given once the route is assigned. The program allows a large number of possible routes to be defined.

Alterations in route definitions can be formulated to represent management action as well. For example, suppose in our hypothetical area we want to examine the implications of introducing duplicate trail segments over certain portions of an area. This investment policy's implications for congestion can be incorporated into the model by defining alternative routes to get to the same point. In terms of figure 2.2, if the added segment is to parallel segment 2, then there are at least two ways to get to campsite 3 when entering at $E1$. That is, the added way calls for moving along the new segment (say, 12) in the one direction. Thus modifications in, or enlargement of, the trail network can play an important role in defining a class of managerial strategies. The simulator can be used to help investigate the consequences of such strategies in advance of introduction. More campsites may also be entered and represented by expanding the set of routes in a similar fashion.

Once the set of routes is defined, they must be assigned to the parties. As we have noted, there are three important factors for this assignment process. The first is the time of day (i.e., a.m. versus p.m.) when the party is scheduled to enter the area. The second is the mode of travel of the party. In specifying this influence we have assumed that riders may select routes different from those chosen by hiking parties. There are any number of reasons why this pattern may be different across these two groups, but it need not be different. Empirical information can be utilized to distinguish these patterns. Equally important, this factor allows the manager to examine the implications of restricting the use of certain portions of the area to parties that are hiking as opposed to riding. Finally, the program distinguishes route selection by designated week-types. That is, each week of the simulation can be designated a type and this classification will affect the routes which can be selected within that week. This latter conditioning variable was selected to capture the effects of weather conditions on use patterns. During certain portions of the season, some areas may be closed because they are inaccessible. In total, the program allows for twelve different assignment schemes—a breakdown by time, mode of travel and week-type (i.e., $2 \times 2 \times 3 = 12$).

The process of assignment is probabilistic. Reference is made to one of twelve conditional cumulative probability distributions based on the characteristics of the party and its time of arrival, both in terms of hour of the day and week of the simulation run. Based on these prespecified discrete probability distributions, one route is assigned to each party, and this determines its travel behavior during its presence in the area.

2.5 RECORDING ENCOUNTERS

Two basic types of encounters are distinguished in the program's recording of events during the simulation. These are trail and camp encounters. Each of these meetings is just what the name implies, that is, trail encounters refer to the meetings a party has with other parties while on trail segments in the area. The model has great flexibility in further subdividing this set. First, the encounters are distinguished by the parties encountered. That is, account is taken of the size and mode of travel of the party encountered. Moreover, since these meetings can occur in either of two ways, a further distinction can be made. Parties moving in opposite directions along a given trail segment will necessarily meet, and these are designated meeting trail encounters. Additionally, since the mode of travel will affect the speed of the party, it is possible that one or more parties may pass a given party while it is traversing a given segment. These trail encounters can be distinguished from meeting encounters and are designated overtaking encounters.

There are important reasons for making these distinctions. Recall that the rationale for keeping track of encounters stems from the objective of recording disruptions to a recreationist's solitude while he is participating in low-density recreation. These intrusions may have different severity, and one way of approximating this effect is to suggest that it is related to the time that the individual perceives the presence of others. In the case of meeting encounters, parties are moving in opposite directions, so that this time interval will be shorter than for the case of overtaking encounters. Clearly, the quantitative importance of these two types of trail encounters is an empirical question. We cannot test for these differences on the basis of existing information. However, the simulation model provides the program user the ability to make a distinction in the event that future research identifies significant differences.

The specific logic utilized to tally the encounters represents a rather innovative structuring of the simulation language GPSS V. Each trail segment in the area has associated with it two "groups," one for each direction of movement along the segment. Each party in the area at any moment in time must be a member of only one of these groups or in camp. Figure 2.3 illustrates schematically the group concept. The "stick men" represent parties which are uniquely identified by indexes assigned to them when they entered the system. In the terminology of GPSS, these parties are called transactions and they carry with them certain descriptive parameters, which identify among other things their mode of travel, size, and route designation. In figure 2.3, group 1 for segment 10 indicates one direction on this segment and group 2 the opposite. The groups contain the indexes, which in turn allows the program to reference the parametric information associated with the party and thereby distinguish the type and size of both the encountered party and the encountering party.

Since the logic of the encounter routine is unique, it may be desirable to review it. Recall that the program is event driven, so that when a party is going to change its state (i.e., enter or leave the system, a trail segment, or a campsite), an event occurs which activates the record keeping. The following steps are performed whenever a party enters a trail segment. First, in its simplest form the recording of meeting encounters requires note be taken of the "group" that the entering party has joined. Then the program increases all parties in the opposite "group's" meeting encounter count parameter by one. Moreover, the meeting encounter count parameter is incremented by the number of parties in the opposing group. Overtaking encounters require the following steps: (1) calculating the segment departure time of all parties already in the same "group" of the entering party, (2) determining the departure time of the entering party, (3) comparing these times and incrementing the overtaking encounter count parameter of each member of the group having the same or later time scheduled for exit from the segment, and (4) increasing the entering party's overtaking encounter count parameter by the total number of these parties.

Actually, the preceding logic summarizes the essentials of the trail encounter routine. Since we do make the distinction between the mode of

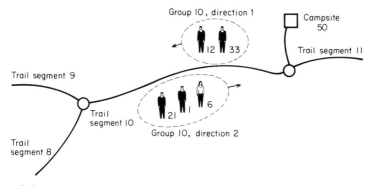

Figure 2.3

travel and the size of the encountered party, these count parameters are more disaggregated, but this explanation serves to capture the essentials of the logic.

Camp encounters are recorded in a single "group" concept. Each party in a given camp belongs to one group and the entrance of a new party to that camp increments the camp encounter count parameters of each party already in the group by one and the entering party by the total number of these parties. The number of nights in which a party had at least one camp encounter is also recorded. The latter provides some indication of the distribution of the camp encounters over the nights of a party's total trip. This is accomplished by setting up a control variable which is set equal to one each time a party has a camp encounter. Thus, if in the course of one night the party has ten camp encounters or one, this variable will remain one. Should the party have no camp encounters, it will retain its initial value of zero. When the party leaves the camp, this variable is added to the count parameter for nights of camp encounters.

Each time an event takes place in the system, the parameters of the parties directly or indirectly involved in the event will be updated, and the clock advanced. Needless to say, the event-driven approach to simulation is more efficient in its utilization of computer time for simulation runs.

2.6   DATA GENERATED WITHIN THE PROGRAM

It is not difficult to realize that the outline of the logic of the operation of this program is only one of the difficult questions which had to be resolved in its design. An equally important aspect of the program is its record keeping. There are vast quantities of information that might be tabulated in any simulation run. What information can be maintained and presented in a convenient framework?

Before this question can be resolved, it is necessary to recognize that the recorded encounters are random variables. Probabilistic decisions and variables are an integral part of the simulation model so that identical input data and alternative sequences of pseudorandom numbers are likely to give different recorded encounter variables. Thus the model describes a stochastic process, and to estimate the implications of any action, we need to run the experiment several times in order to learn something of the distribution of our estimates. If our primary interest is in the central tendency of the distribution of average encounters an individual might expect during a trip of preassigned length, then an increased number of independent replications of each experiment will serve to "reduce" the variance in our estimates of the expected encounters. It should be noted that the variation involved here is the between-replication variation and results from the stochastic nature of the model. There is also variation in the

experiences of the parties in a given run. This variation is due only in part
to the influence of random factors. It is also the result of the size and mode
of travel of the party, and the route it takes while in the area. Both sources
of variation must be dealt with in analyzing the results of the simulation
model.

The output of the model is available for each party which entered the
area and consists of its encounter record, characteristics, and route pattern.
Moreover, these data have been aggregated in several ways. First, the
records of parties by their mode of travel and size have been aggregated;
thus we can calculate the experiences of all small hiking parties or all
medium-sized riding parties. Table 2.1 illustrates one such table. Alternatively, these data are aggregated according to the length in days of the
trips taken by the parties in the area. Thus we can calculate the average
experience of all parties who took one-day trips. Table 2.2 illustrates this
type of table.

Two important variations on these basic tables are also available. In
order to describe them, it is necessary to provide some background. Managers of wilderness areas as well as wilderness enthusiasts have suggested
that those encounters which occur on the segments a party must take to
enter or leave an area are anticipated and therefore do not represent serious
disruptions of the solitude of the experience. While there is no empirical
evidence to support this observation, the program has been designed to
allow the researcher to designate a subset of all trail segments as entry or
exit segments and record the encounters occurring on these segments
separately. Tables corresponding to 2.1 and 2.2 are available for these
peripheral segments.

It is important to be able to identify those trail segments or camps which
are most heavily utilized in the area. The program does this by recording
the encounters by trail segment and campsite. That is, it keeps a count of
the encounters which occur by type on each segment and campsite in the
area.

In order to be able to assess the status of the area in terms of entries
and exits, a table records the arrivals and departures by the mode of travel
of the party during each day of the simulated season. Finally, in order that
the correspondence between desired distribution of users by type, time
schedule, and route might be checked, the actual generation frequencies
for the parties are recorded and tabulated.

2.7   SUMMARY

This chapter has outlined the workings and implicitly the data
necessary to construct a traffic simulation model of any low-density recreational area. In the next chapter we discuss the question of data collected
external to the model and the modeling of the wilderness trail system. Since

the model describes a stochastic process, estimates of the kind of experience an individual recreationist might expect under alternative conditions such as levels of total use of the area or character of the time patterns of arrivals necessarily requires multiple runs of each scenario. Chapter 4 will discuss this problem in more detail.

REFERENCES

Cicchetti, C. J. and V. K. Smith. 1973. "Congestion, Quality Deterioration, and Optimal Use: Wilderness Recreation in the Spanish Peaks Primitive Area," *Social Science Research,* vol. 2 (March).

Fisher, A. C. and J. V. Krutilla. 1972. "Determination of Optimal Capacity of Resource-Based Recreation Facilities," *Natural Resources Journal,* vol. 72, no. 3.

Naylor, T. H. 1971. *Computer Simulation Experiments with Models of Economic Systems* (New York: John Wiley & Sons).

Stankey, G. H. 1971. "The Perception of Wilderness Recreation Carrying Capacity: A Geographic Study in Natural Resources Management," (Ph.D. dissertation, Michigan State Univ.).

———. 1972. "A Strategy for the Definition and Management of Wilderness Quality," in *Natural Environments: Studies in Theoretical and Applied Analysis,* edited by J. V. Krutilla (Baltimore: Johns Hopkins University Press for Resources for the Future).

TABLE 2.1. Encounters by Party Type — An Example

Party Type-Size	Number of Parties	Trail Encounters						Camp Encounters Number
		Hiking Parties			Riding Parties			
		S	M	L	S	M	L	
Hiking Parties								
Small (S)	9	0	8	1	2	4	6	13
Medium (M)	36	34	34	5	4	23	28	62
Large (L)	5	1	5	0	0	3	3	5
Riding Parties								
Small (S)	4	2	4	0	0	3	5	12
Medium (M)	20	4	23	3	3	14	25	53
Large (L)	26	6	28	3	5	25	30	70

Note: This table is presented for example only and is based on experiments with a small hypothetical wilderness area. See V.K. Smith, D. Webster and N. Heck, "A Prototype Simulation Model of A Wilderness Area," Operational Research Quarterly, December 1974. It reports the average of ten replications rounded to whole numbers, of a simulation run with a four-week season in which 100 parties entered the area.

TABLE 2.2.　Encounters by Trip Length — An Example

Length of Trip (Days)	Number of Parties	Trail Encounters						Camp Encounters	
		Hiking Parties			Riding Parties			Number	Nights
		S	M	L	S	M	L		
1	31	6	29	5	3	15	22	–	
2	63	14	65	8	11	53	70	183	50
3	6	1	8	0	1	3	4	31	9

See note a to Table 2.1 for a description of the source of the data.

CHAPTER 3

CODING THE SPANISH PEAKS WILDERNESS AREA: PREPARATION OF INPUT INFORMATION

3.1 INTRODUCTION

In chapter 2 we described a model for simulating the recreational traffic flows and patterns in wilderness areas. Our objective was to learn something about the effects of such travel behavior on an individual party of recreationists. Specifically, how do other users affect the frequency of encounters a party can anticipate for a given wilderness outing? Such a model is useful for managerial and planning purposes only if it is capable of accommodating the traffic flows and patterns in an actual wilderness area. While it is true that the conceptual framework may be helpful in thinking about the problem, it is also clear that the model can be useful only as it is parameterized to represent a specific case. In this chapter we outline the process by which we defined a simulation model (i.e., estimated the required input data) for a specific case, the Spanish Peaks Wilderness Area.

As we noted in chapter 2, there are four steps in the simulation of wilderness recreation in a given area: (1) scheduling, (2) characterizing, (3) routing, and (4) recording. In each of the first three stages, it is necessary to provide information to the model on the "how to" of the process. That is, the specific plan of action must be defined for the process to, in effect, play out the scenario. The last step is the data collection phase, and generally a common set of information is required for any area.[1] While the characteristics, both in terms of use patterns and area network, will be greatly different from one wilderness facility to the next, we can expect the basic process of wilderness travel behavior to remain invariant.

Basically, within the set of input data there are two different kinds of information required. One relates to, or describes the physical characteristics of the wilderness area in question, while the other describes the user

---

[1] This statement assumes that there is a uniform management policy established for all wilderness and roadless areas so that the recreational service flows provided by these areas can be evaluated with the same types of data.

characteristics, including their modes of travel and party sizes, their arrival pattern, and their routes of travel within the area. It should also be noted that these two types of data interact, in that the patterns of movement and the speeds of a given type (i.e., mode of travel and size) party will be affected by the physical characteristics of the area in question. For example, small riding parties may be capable of rather rapid travel if trails are of gentle grade and in good condition. A variation in either of these conditions may reduce travel speed considerably.

In what follows we review the input data in the order in which they are necessary to our simulation model. The first two sets of these can be discussed rather quickly. These concern the scheduling and characterizing of the parties coming to the area. As we noted in chapter 2, the first step is to designate the length of time of the simulation run, in weeks. A four-week run was selected for our purposes. Two considerations were important in our decision. First, the daily use pattern was such that arrivals peaked over the weekend. Moreover, several of the parties selected extended trips into the area (in some cases as long as seven days). Both considerations required a period of several weeks in order that some of these parties would be able to complete their trips and that the effects of weekend use patterns would be reflected. The second consideration was computer cost. All else being equal (including the frequency of arrivals), the longer the simulation run, the greater the computational cost. It should also be noted that since the period is representative of use patterns throughout the season, it is not clear that a longer time period for the simulation run provides any more information on the expected experience.[2] The total number of parties using the area was consistent with the postulated level of seasonal utilization. In the next chapter we discuss our "base-case" or frame of reference simulation run, in which the number of parties for this experiment was representative of the 1970 season. A part of the remaining data, which we shall discuss in what follows, is based on sample information from some 600 parties using the Spanish Peaks Wilderness Area during the 1970 recreational season. While this survey was conducted primarily for other research purposes, parties were nonetheless requested to provide information which was also useful for our model.

The distribution of use across the four weeks of each run was specified to designate either existing patterns or in some cases to represent the results of a postulated managerial policy, such as advance registration. More specific details on these data are provided in the chapters that follow. The daily distribution was also either based on the available data or altered to depict managerial policy. Finally, in the absence of specific data, the

---

[2] It should, however, be noted that if the managerial objective is concerned with the within-group variation as well as the expected experience, then a longer time period for the season with more parties may provide a better estimate of the variation across parties during a given replication of the model.

distribution of arrivals by time of day was developed on the basis of the informed judgment of those familiar with the area.[3]

The assignment of characteristics to these parties was based on the relative frequencies of user types in our sample. Thus the mode of travel (i.e., backpacker versus horserider) and the size of the party were based on the sample information. It should be noted that this sample information served to define the population proportions (i.e., probability a party was a backpacker, etc.), with the specific assignment being done probabilistically for each individual party.

Given this information, it is necessary to translate the physical characteristics of the area and its specific use pattern into a form that is acceptable to the model. That is, in regard to the physical characteristics of the wilderness area under examination, we shall want to know such things as the nature and extent of the trail system, i.e., we will need a description of the network of nodes or potential decision points such as trail heads, trail bifurcations, campsites, places of changes in gradients or other trail conditions that might affect the rate of movement. In what follows we discuss the components that are required to route parties that have been scheduled and characterized.

3.2 MODELING THE TRAIL SYSTEM

When working with "on the ground" features of an area, the relevant information must be taken literally off the ground. Fortunately, in many cases this information has been assembled in one form or another by others who have been on the ground in the area. For example, the U.S. Forest Service typically has, or intends to develop, a management plan for each of its wilderness or primitive areas, and where these plans have been developed, much of the relevant data can be found already compiled. Similarly, one can generally obtain from the U.S. Geological Survey suitable topographic maps that will provide a great deal of the necessary data in more or less adequate detail. But, whatever the advantages of getting data readily in hand to undertake the kind of desk calculations necessary for preparing input data, it is ultimately necessary to field check such information if a high degree of accuracy of input information is to be obtained. Several arguments can be advanced for the field survey ultimately if really accurate data are to be obtained for the simulator.

Often the basic data on which the USGS topographic maps have been developed were collected some time ago, and in the interim many changes that are not reflected on the maps can have taken place. The USGS 15-minute series Spanish Peaks Quadrangle, for example, is based on data obtained from aerial photographs taken in 1947 and field checked in 1950.

[3] In this regard Robert Lucas and George Stankey have been especially helpful in the setting of those variables for the area which had to be based on judgment.

A number of things have occurred in the intervening years to alter the trail system in localized areas, which raises questions about the accuracy of some of the trails shown by the topographic map of the area. For example, it is not uncommon for packers and outfitters to set off cross country to bring their clients to a nontrail-serviced area. Or, a new trail may be cut because an existing trail laid out by the Forest Service for administrative purposes is not attractive for recreation. A packer's trail may also be preferred by wilderness travelers on foot, and over time, a segment of the trail system that is not reflected on the USGS topographic maps may become established. The Forest Service may wish to close out some trails and add others, events which would not be reflected on the maps until the area was rephotographed.

The problems resulting from the changes that are not reflected on the official USGS maps can be overcome provided there are recently compiled data on the trail system in the management plans prepared for such areas. One difficulty results, particularly in "horse country," or where a great deal of travel is done on horseback, when the management plans may list and locate campsites that can accommodate a large horseparty—and overlook a number of very attractive, small campsites fully adequate to service backpackers simply because the area is insufficiently large to pasture horses. In short, a careful review of what is on the ground both in terms of the trail network and the identification of campsites (designated, if necessary, as to whether for foot travelers only, or for horseback) should be undertaken to make certain of the accuracy of the trail network input data. As we noted in chapter 2, the only record of an area's trail system which is available to the model is derived from the defined routes taken in the area. Consequently, such careful inventory of the physical characteristics of trail segments and campsites will be extremely useful in checking the defined routes. While these routes are likely to be based on the patterns of actual users, it is nonetheless important to judge whether those cases where there is limited sample information are representative of established route plans.

Assuming, however, that adequate published or other primary source data can be obtained through Forest Service management plans in combination with USGS topographic maps, how is this information to be treated to prepare it for use with the simulator? Several things must be done to take information readily observed from maps and lists and prepare it in a form suitable for coding for computer use.

First, it is necessary to transform a visual display of trails on a map into some indexing scheme. What is important here is that it be done in a manner that will be most useful in obtaining information relevant for other elements of the computational problem. Presumably, therefore, we would like to note all of the decision nodes in the system, such as trail heads, branches, and campsites—all features around which decisions can revolve. Second, we might appreciate that intranodal segments may have non-decision features which nonetheless have significance for the informational inputs to the simulator. For example, between any two campsites, trail branches, or between a trail branch and campsite, there may be sharp changes in trail gradients that would alter the expected rate of travel, or a scenic overlook that can be expected to stop parties with a given probability and average delay. These features should be noted for purposes of ultimately developing an expected average rate of speed for every segment and subsegment of the trail system.

Figure 3.1 represents the Spanish Peaks Wilderness Area trail network transposed onto a calibrated grid that permits easier location of points along trail segments and other distance-related features. The number 1 marks the Spanish Creek trail head while numbers 2, 5, and 6, for example, identify trail bifurcations. All of these locations represent decision nodes in the network, for each will represent an option about which a conscious choice must be made. The decision regarding the Spanish Peaks entry point doubtless reflects a conscious choice regarding a particular trip plan which, if it includes nodes 5 and 6, obviously involves a decision to proceed along a route partially defined by the 5–6 nodes rather than the alternate branch, i.e., the segment defined by the 5–16 nodes.

Consider next the segment of the trail system between the 6 and 7 nodes. Here is a situation in which there are both decision nodes (trail branches and campsites) and intranodal trail gradient changes that require attention if an accurate estimate of transit times is to be made.[4] Beginning at the point marked by number 6, we note from the topographic map changes in the gradient along this trail segment. From research done on the relation between backpackers' rate of speed as a function of elevation gain (Cunningham, 1971), we would judge that there would be changes in rate of speed (measuring from 6) at trail miles 0.7, 1.7, 1.9, 2.1, 2.3, and 3.5, at intranodal points which we may designate as 6.1, 6.2, S9 (Mirror Lake Campsite at TM 1.9), 6.3, 6.4, and 6.5. For ease in illustration we put this information into a tabular form similar to the manner in which the entire trail network was treated in developing the data input for the simulator. In table 3.1 we note the node, trail mile, and the estimated rate of speed in travel (different for different directions of travel) on the intranodal segments having different trail gradients.

While it is necessary to go through this step in assembling information in order to prepare the data ultimately for computer input, the characteristics of the simulation model require that the data on travel speed be converted into the time required to traverse a trail segment, or for the sake of brevity, transit time. The tabular presentation in table 3.2 illustrates the form in which these data were prepared for coding for direct computer input.

---

[4] See appendix 3.A.

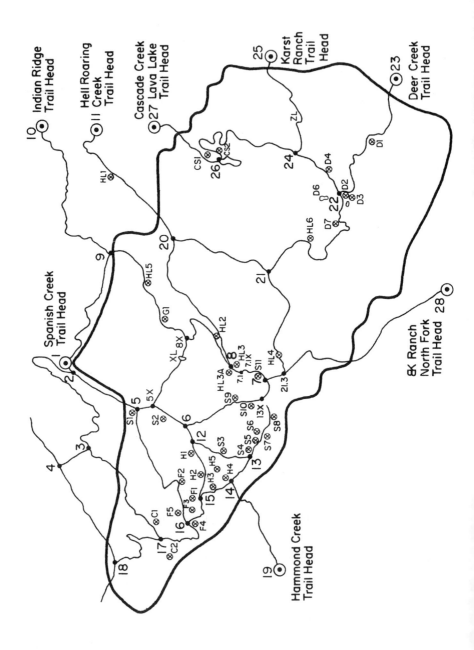

Figure 3.1

One point deserves to be made at this juncture. While it was essential to break down the trail segments in the intranodal range at points where changes in trail gradients would alter the expected rate of speed, once the segment length measured in miles (or fractions thereof) was divided by the travel speed in miles per hour, to get the transit time, all of the intranodal segments could be telescoped, and their transit times simply aggregated.[5] For example, between the trail branch at 6 and the Mirror Lake campsite at S9, a distance of 3.3 miles, three intranodal segments on which the travel rate differs can be distinguished. One cannot go directly from point 6 to S9 without getting a weighted average travel speed from which to obtain the transit time for the 3.3-mile distance. This, of course, can be obtained directly from table 3.2, by simply adding the individual transit times, i.e., 35, 70.6, and 6.9 minutes, or 112.5 minutes, as the transit time for the total 6–S9 intranodal segment. The advantage of collapsing the subsegments stems from the control mechanism for the simulation model. Recall that in chapter 2 we noted that the model was event driven, so that data are collected whenever a party changes its status (i.e., an event takes place). Thus a party's entering or leaving a campsite or trail segment is an event. Consequently, the fewer the number of defined trail segments, the fewer will be the potential events and hence the more economical the operation of the simulator.

In conducting the empirical research on the trail system, it was initially desirable to identify each decision node in the trail network using some of the campsite designators presented in the proposed wilderness management plan for the Spanish Peaks. This was useful in identifying intranodal trail segments for travel speed and transit time calculations. The logic of the simulator and the programming language in which it is written, however, require a very specific form for conveying such information for computer processing. What is required by the computer model is that all segments be numbered, with campsites being considered also as segments, but of zero length. The system is then described by assigning an identification number to every segment of trail (including intervening campsites), usually for convenience in some logically ordered progression, i.e., the sequence of numbers corresponding to the position of the trail segments. The program requires that the direction of travel be indicated in order to use the corresponding transit time, and that campsites be distinguished from trail segments. Accordingly, as we noted in chapter 2, direction of travel along the segments is indicated by either 1 or 2, while a segment number corresponding to a campsite is given a numeral 3, appended as the terminal digit of the segment number.

Consider, for example, the coding of that portion of a route that happened to fall between the node designator 6 and the campsite node S9 of

[5] See, for example, appendix 3.B.

table 3.2. Suppose that the trail segment numbers corresponding to the intranodal segments 6.0–6.1, 6.1–6.2, 6.2–S9 were, as they happen to be in the Spanish Peaks coded data set, respectively 078, 079, 080, and 081. Accordingly, if a given party were proceeding from node 6 to the campsite at Mirror Lake designated as S9, the information coded for computer use would take the following form: 1,0781 / 2,0791 / 3,0801 / 4,0813 / 5,9999. The number 1 appearing as the last digit of each trail segment group indicates that the transit time relevant to the case is obtained from the column in table 3.2 reading downward. Of course, the number 3 appearing as the terminal digit in the fourth coded group indicates that segment 81 happens to be a campsite. If the direction of travel were from the campsite at Mirror Lake to, say, node 6, the information prepared for the computer would take an alternative form in the terminal digit, i.e., 1,0813 / 2,0802 / 3,0792 / 4,0782 / 5,9999. Step 5 in each case with the 9999 designator is required simply to indicate the end of the route (see Wilderness Area Simulation Model User's Manual IBM-RFF 1973 N.T.I.S. Accession No. PB 233 364/AS for details).

In the context of our programming language, each sequence of trail segments and campsites is designated a function.[6] Hence when a party selects a particular route, the program mimics this behavior through the use of the corresponding function to describe all the "events" relevant to that party. The material to this point must be assembled in order to provide (1) a basis for the definition of the routes; and (2) estimates of the time required to traverse defined trail segments according to the direction of movement. Two more steps are necessary if the process of routing is to be parameterized. First, the routes themselves must be defined. And second, the probability distributions conditioned on party type, time of arrival, and type of week must be estimated. As we noted in chapter 2, if all screening dimensions are considered important, there are twelve such distributions which would need to be estimated.

Before proceeding to a discussion of these last two steps in the routing of a party, some additional information on the definition of transit times for each party is necessary. The estimates of the rate of speed of travel, and hence indirectly the transit time for any segment of the trail system, is a reference average speed of travel for a single person, or small hiking, party. Therefore, there are two sources of potential variation in the estimated transit time. One relates to the characteristics of the party—whether traveling by foot or on horseback. The other relates to various random elements attending travel that will make the travel speed vary over a given segment, not only among parties of the same type, but also between one time and another for the same party.

[6] See *Wilderness Area Simulation Model,* User's Manual. N.T.I.S. Accession No. PB 233 364/AS.

Considering the first source of variation, we know that small parties typically travel faster than large parties simply because there are non-coincident distractions that afflict travelers, and the larger the party the more frequent will be the interruptions to travel. Secondly, typically and particularly in mountainous terrain, travel on horseback is faster than travel on foot. Accordingly, for this reason it is necessary to provide for variation in travel speeds among parties, depending on size and travel mode. Table 3.3 gives the reference transit time multiplier for this purpose. Appendix 3.A provides a sketch map of the Spanish Peaks trail system and tables of the transit times for the trail segments noting direction for small hiking parties.

We have assumed that a second source of variability will serve to capture some of the conventional random elements found in such circumstances. To incorporate these into the assigned transit speed for any given party traversing any given trail segment, we assume that the transit time for a party on a given segment is normally distributed, with a mean corresponding to the adjusted value estimated for the appropriate segment and direction. The adjustment reflects the mode of travel and size of the party, as we have just noted. The variation about this central tendency is expressed as a percent of the mean and is fixed for all parties and segments. That is, the standard deviation relative to the mean (i.e., coefficient of variation) is assumed to be constant across trail segments and party types. Algebraically the model serves to define transit time as follows:

$$y_{ij} = (x_i T_j)(1 + ku)$$

where y_{ij} represents the jth party type traversing the ith segment, x_i represents the ith segment's reference transit time, T_j represents the reference time modifier relevant to party type j, k is the ratio of standard deviation to mean for all segments and parties, and u represents the random variability about the transit speed, assumed to be normally distributed with mean zero and standard deviation of one. This procedure yields an actual transit time, y_{ij}, which varies normally about the mean, μ_{ij}, with a standard deviation of k percent of the mean.

Consider then an example where we take a small horseparty moving between nodes 6.0 and 6.1 with transit times of 35 minutes in the 1 direction (see table 3.2) and assume k is 3 percent. The transit time for our y_{ij} would then begin with the reference transit time of $(x_j =)$ 35 minutes, multiplied by the modifier $(T_j =)$ 0.8, whose product in turn is multiplied by one plus 0.03 times a pseudorandom number u generated by a computer subroutine for the standard normal distribution function. Assume that for this event (i.e., horseparty moving between nodes 6.0 and 6.1) the computer draws a value $u = -0.90$. Then,

$$y_{ij} = 35 \times 0.8 \times [1.0 + 0.03(-0.90)] = 28.0(1.0 - 0.027) = 27.2$$

The mean transit time, μ_{ij}, is 28 minutes. However, the actual transit time y_{ij} is 27.2 minutes for this particular party.

Something might be said about our evaluation of the accuracy of these data. Work on the trail system proceeded with USGS topographic maps, with reference to the proposed "Spanish Peaks Wilderness" draft plan for the area's management, and with a week in the field to check the data obtained from interpretation of primary source data. The area's boundaries and trail network, including trail modification, and inventory of campsites presented in the management plan served as a basic source which, in conjunction with the topographic maps, provided information on trail gradients and related physical features. Nevertheless, it was discovered that much additional refinement was possible by checking transit times in the field, observing potential backpack campsites that were overlooked in the management plan, presumably because the USFS staff assigned to the task implicitly had in mind campsites providing pasture, an essential criterion for horseparties, but of limited relevance for backpackers. One has a strong impression that a substantially larger number of campsites are available to accommodate at least the small and even medium-sized backpack parties than are revealed by the USFS staff inventory, or that could be uncovered during a week's reconnaissance in the field. It should be noted, however, that if a systematically conducted intensive inventory of potential small party backpack campsites were discovered, these could be incorporated into the trail system through a redefinition of the routes for the area.

There is also a certain skepticism regarding accuracy of travel speeds and transit times. These were originally taken from research reported on by Cunningham (1971), and served as the basis for our desk calculations. Data by Cunningham were presented in terms of the relation between minutes needed to travel 1 mile and feet of altitude gained per mile. The relation between speed of travel upon ascending on the one hand, or descending on the other, however, is a rather complex one. Movement along a good trail of moderate grade will show a moderately faster rate of travel moving down the trail than when moving up a positive, even though moderate, incline. With very steep grades, particularly over rough trails, however, the speed of travel in descending may not be any faster than in ascending. While a rough feel for these relationships was obtained by making checks of different gradients and other trail conditions in the field, there is no question that a fuller investigation of these relationships would produce better data.

The data on the relative rates of speed, given party size and mode of travel, were obtained by discussions with knowledgeable persons who had vast experience with wilderness travel, both afoot and on horseback, and with both small private parties and large organized pack trips. On the basis of judgment arrived at in this fashion, we concluded that a medium-sized party would typically move 10 percent slower than a single or small-sized party, and a large party as much as 20 percent slower than an individual or small-sized party. Similarly, we assumed that particularly in mountainous terrain, a hiking or backpacking party would take roughly 20 percent more time to traverse a given trail segment than a horseback party of corresponding size. These happen to be no more than informed judgments, but whether it is worth mounting a considerable effort to refine these data will depend upon how critical the difference in the data will be for the results in evaluating the congestion phenomenon and its operational measure (the expected frequency of encounter). This question can be answered by running some sensitivity tests based on the assumptions of travel speed differences to determine the effect on the measured outcomes (chapter 5, p. 121). If the differences are inconsequential, there is no need for a large resource or investigative input to refine these data. If the conclusions regarding encounters, hence congestion, tend to be sensitive with respect to our assumptions on travel speeds and the differences in speed among different size parties and travel modes, then obviously that area of empirical research must receive further attention.

3.3 ROUTE DEFINITION AND SELECTION

The routes in the Spanish Peaks Area were defined on the basis of sketch maps provided by some 600 parties using the facility during the 1970 recreational season. These parties were requested to show by arrows the route taken within the area, marking the campsites occupied with an "X" along with the number of nights spent at each campsite. Additional questions included in the accompanying questionnaire provided such information as the date of entry, number in the party, mode of travel, number of days out, and a variety of other incidental (to our purpose) data. Figure 3.2 illustrates one such sketch map.

Of the 600-odd questionnaires with requested information on routes selected, roughly 400 were returned with sufficiently accurate information to be useful. These sketch maps were then sorted out to identify characteristic routes, with a route being defined not only in terms of entry point, trail segments, and campsites occupied, but also differentiated by number of nights spent at each site and number of days out in total. Sufficient variation in "routes" thus defined was found to permit identifying 104 "characteristic routes." These 104 characteristic routes were then all coded as indicated previously. Appendix 3.C provides a listing of these routes in alpha-numeric form to conform to the map of the area in appendix 3.A.

Ideally, we would have liked to have each party using the wilderness area during a survey season maintain a journal giving information on the

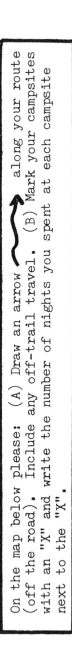

On the map below please: (A) Draw an arrow ↗ along your route (off the road). Include any off-trail travel. (B) Mark your campsites with an "X" and write the number of nights you spent at each campsite next to the "X".

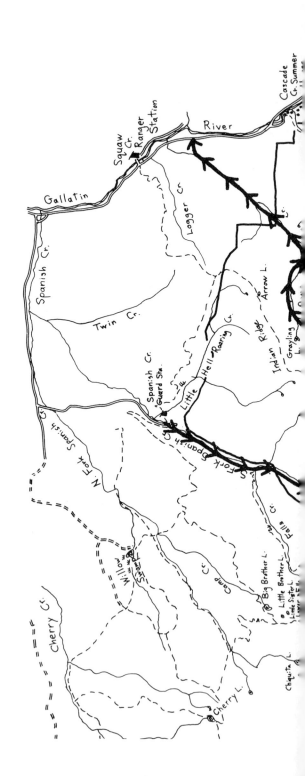

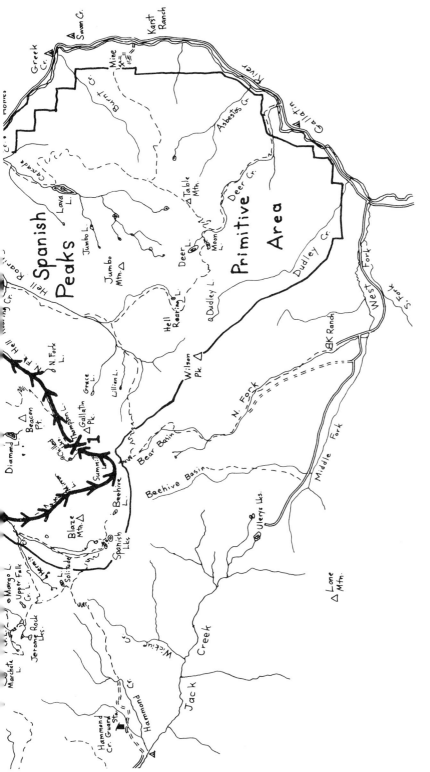

Figure 3.2

time of arrival, both as to hour of day, day of week, and week of season; the trail head entry point; time spent on each trail segment in the intra-nodal segments; time of arrival at camp of occupance; time of departure, and so on. Perhaps, should information of that detailed accuracy be shown to be important, i.e., the simulated frequency of encounters being sensitive to slight variation in such detail, an appropriately selected sample of such users might be requested to participate in the research effort.[7] For the Spanish Peaks prototype effort, neither time nor circumstances permitted obtaining data that detailed.

Given these route definitions, there remains the problem of specifying the probability of a party selecting any one of them. In chapter 2 these probabilities were assumed to be a function of: (1) the time of arrival, whether morning or afternoon; (2) the mode of travel of the party; and (3) the type of week defined. While we do not have empirical evidence, it is probably reasonable to suggest that the first two of these variables are the most important. Consequently, we attempted to estimate, using our sample, the users' conditional probability distributions for route selection based on the mode of travel and the time of arrival. Unfortunately, this implies that four distributions had to be derived. Since there are 104 routes and only 400 observations, the cell frequencies become too low to suggest that we have reasonable estimates of these relative frequencies.[8] Conse-quently, we were forced to assume that the time of arrival was not im-portant to the route selection and we differentiated the distributions ac-cording to the mode of travel of the arriving party. These distributions were derived by calculating the relative frequency with which each type of party (i.e., hiker versus rider) in our sample selected each route. Appendix 3.D reports these estimated probability distributions.

Several points should be noted concerning our route probability distri-butions. In some cases (notably routes 2, 14, 15, 18, 40, 43, 44, and others) neither hikers nor riders have a nonzero probability of selecting the routes. This would appear to contradict our previous statements that

[7] A full-scale cooperative research and management effort is being conducted (1974–75) using the Desolation Wilderness. Users maintain a trip diary in simplified format to record actual experience in those respects.

[8] Since we did not have information to estimate the probability of route given ar-rival time, we utilized the relationship between joint and conditional probabilities. That is, we could estimate the probability of any group (i.e., hiking parties or riding parties) selecting a route from our data [i.e., $P(R)$]. Moreover, from the character of the routes themselves and knowledge of the use patterns for the area, we can set the probability of arriving in the a.m. or p.m. given a particular route [i.e., $P(T/R = \bar{R})$]. Consequently, we have the probability of a route and time [i.e., $P(T$ and $R) = P(T/R) \times P(R)$]. Our setting of the arrival time distribution during the day gives us $P(T)$, hence the required conditional probability $P(R/T)$ can be derived as:

$$P(R/T) = \frac{P(R \text{ and } T)}{P(T)} = \frac{P(T/R) \times P(R)}{P(T)}$$

these distributions are data based. The problem arises in rounding the relative frequencies to tenths of a percent. Parties did in fact select the routes we have enumerated. However, in some cases only one or two of the 400 parties selected the route. Hence we have several cases where routes have been defined but will not be selected with our probability distributions.

It is also important to note that we would have preferred estimates of these distributions, which reflect the time of arrival. Presumably registration at the trail head, along with a request of a sketch map and questionnaire on exit, would provide the data necessary for refinement.

3.4 SUMMARY

This chapter has outlined the principal components in the data preparations necessary to parameterize the model for the Spanish Peaks Wilderness Area. It should be emphasized that our descriptions of the user-based data (i.e., probabilities of party types, sizes, routes) are estimated from questionnaires which were designed primarily to serve objectives other than parameterizing a simulation model of the area. With a better understanding of the degree of refinement required of the data obtained from this prototype effort on the Spanish Peaks, a more adequate set of data can be developed to serve the specific needs of the simulation model. Then the model can be used to address actual management problems, whether involving the Spanish Peaks or other wilderness areas.

REFERENCES

Cunningham, G. A. 1971. "Wilderness Gateway," *Better Camping* (February).
IBM-RFF, Wilderness Area Simulation Model User's Manual. N.T.I.S. Accession No. PB 233 364/AS.
Plan for the Management-Development-Administration of the Spanish Peaks Wilderness (Proposed), undated draft.
Transportation Analysis Procedures for National Forest Planning, Project Report, prepared for the U.S. Forest Service, University of California, Berkeley, July 1971.

TABLE 3.1.　Trail Data Input

| Trail Segment (6, S9, S10, 7) | | Directional Speed in MPH ------- reading -------- | |
Node	Trail Mile	Down	up
6.0	0		
		1.20	2.50
6.1	0.7		
		0.85	2.65
6.2	1.7		
		1.75	1.75
S9[a]	1.9		
		1.60	1.90
6.3	2.1		
		0.70	2.50
6.4	2.3		
		1.30	2.25
S10[b]	3.0		
		1.30	2.25
6.5	3.5		
		0.70	2.50
7.0	3.8		

[a] Mirror Lake trailside campsite.

[b] Emerald Meadows trailside campsite.

TABLE 3.2.   Transit Time Data Input

Trail Segment (6, S9, S10, 7)		Directional Transit Time (Minutes)	
		------- reading --------	
Node	Trail Mile	down	up
		1	2
6.0	0		
		35.0	16.8
6.1	0.7		
		70.6	22.6
6.2	1.7		
		6.9	6.9
S9[a]	1.9		
		7.5	6.3
6.3	2.1		
		17.1	4.8
6.4	2.3		
		32.3	18.7
S10[b]	3.0		
		23.1	13.3
6.5	3.5		
		25.7	7.2
7.0	3.8		

[a] Mirror Lake trailside campsite.

[b] Emerald Meadows trailside campsite.

TABLE 3.3.   Reference Transit Time Multipliers

Party Size	Reference Time Multiplier
Hiker	
Small	1.0
Medium	1.1
Large	1.2
Rider	
Small	0.8
Medium	0.9
Large	1.0

APPENDIX 3.A

Spanish Peaks Wilderness Expanded Trail System

This appendix presents a sketch of the Spanish Peaks prototype area giving the boundaries of the area, and the trail network, with all of the trail nodes used in preparation of the Spanish Peaks data deck noted. The numerical data corresponding to the sketch map (figure 3.3) provide the information that relates the indicated nodes of the assigned trail segments used in computing the intranodal transit times. The actual data deck used for the simulation runs, however, involved collapsing the intranodal segments by simply adding the transit times within the intranodal range (eliminating the decimal numbers) to give the weighted average transit time for a somewhat compressed trail system (see appendix 3.B). Since the simulator is an "event-driven" model, this was done to reduce the number of points along the trails at which the computer must stop to scan the entire system to check for relevant party position changes, hence encounters. The compressed system achieves about a 25 percent reduction in the number of trail segments, and hence an economy in the operation of the simulator by reducing machine time for any given run. Once the intranodal transit times were obtained and aggregated between each pair of nondecimal numbers, the network trail system had to be renumbered. The coded data for the compressed system, accordingly, is a different set (smaller) than one that would be coded directly from the data sheets given in this appendix. The data are presented in this form, however, to illustrate for the reader more precisely how the information was derived, transformed, and prepared for coding and key punching to prepare the data deck for the Spanish Peaks prototype.

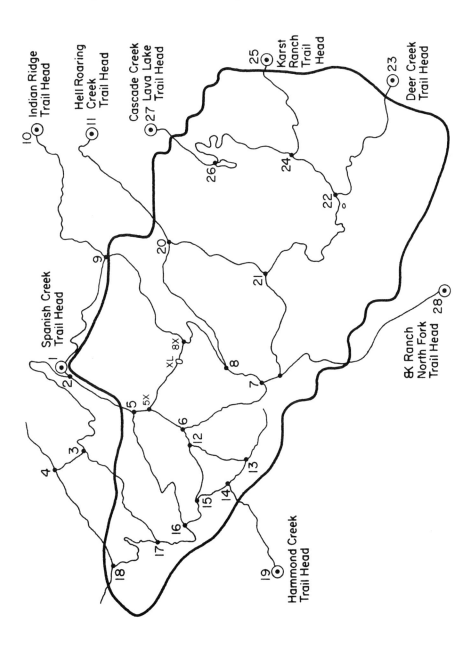

Figure 3.3

Spanish Peaks Wilderness Trail System

Node	Segment	Reference Directional Transit Times in Minutes	
		1	2
1			
	001	11	9
2			
	002	45	38
2.1			
	003	98	82
2.2			
	004	79	66
3			
	005	24	32
4			

No official campsites designated

3			
	006	106	55
3.1			
	007	38	32
3.2			
	008	44	25
C1			
	0093		
C1			
	010	35	20
17			

C1.   Big Brother Lake 0.3 mile s. at TM 4.25.

17			
	011	17	17
17.1			
	012	33	55
17.2			
	013	21	67
17.3			
	014	17	17
18			
	015	91	157
4			

No official campsites designated

Node	Segment	Reference Directional Transit Times in Minutes	
		1	2
17			
	016	21	21
C2			
	0173		
C2			
	018	24	24
F4			
	0193		
F4			
	033	17	17
16			
	021	4	12
F5/F1			
	0223		
F5/F1			
	023	24	24
F2			
	0243		
F2			
	025	9	24
16.1			
	026	34	67
16.2			
	159	34	67
S1			
	0273		
S1			
	028	3	5
5			
	029	3	3
S1'			
	0303		
S1'			
	032	65	72
2			

C2 Marcheta Lake 0.8 miles S.W. of 17 at TM 0.6
F4 Jerome Rock Lakes 0.5 miles S.W. of Trail at TM 1.3
F5 Lower Falls Creek Lake 0.25 miles N.E. of 16 at TM 2.1
F2 Margo Lake 0.2 miles S.E. of Trail at TM 2.8
S1 Trailside Campsite 0.1 miles N.(W) of Trail 5.9
S1' Trailside Campsite opposite S1, small, adjacent to Pioneer Falls

Node	Segment	Reference Directional Transit Times in Minutes	
		1	2
16			
	033	17	17
F3/F4			
	0343/0193		
F3/F4			
	036	31	31
15			
	037	14	14
H3			
	0383		
H3			
	039	2	20
H2			
	0403		
H2			
	041	24	67
H1			
	0423		
H1			
	043	7	20
12			
	044	19	23
6			
	045	22	26
S2			
	0463		
S2			
	047	38	32
5			

F3	Jerome Rock Lakes	Trailside at TM 0.3
F4	Jerome Rock Lakes	Off trail S. 0.3 m. at TM 0.3
F1	Upperfalls Creek L.	Off trail N. 0.3 m. at TM 0.7
H2	Trailsite	Trailside at TM 2.0
H3	(Hermit Trail)	Off trail 0.5 m. at TM 1.7
H1	Trailsite	Trailside at TM 2.7
H5	Hermit Lake	Off trail at TM 2.1
S2	Trailsite	0.2 miles off trail at TM 4.3

Node	Segment	Reference Directional Transit Times in Minutes	
		1	2
15			
	037	14	14
H3			
	0383		
H3			
	050	7	7
H3'			
	0513		
H3'			
	052	14	14
H4			
	053.3		
H4			
	054	7	7
14			
	055	17	17
14.1			
	056	30	30
13			
	057	0	0
S4			
	0583		
S4			
	059	20	40
S3			
	0603		
S3			
	061	33	65
12			
	044	19	23
6			

H3	Trailsite	0.2
H3'	Trailsite	backpacking Site at TM 0.6
H4	Trailsite	0.1 m. N. of Trail at TM 0.8
S4	Trailsite	0.1 m. E. of Trail at TM 2.2
H1	Trailsite	0.3 m. W. of Trail at TM 4.3

Node	Segment	Reference Directional Transit Times in Minutes	
		1	2
13			
S4	057	0	0
S4	0583		
S5	065	14	8
S5	0663		
S6	067	5	3
S6	0683		
S7	069	19	11
S7	0703		
S8	071	34	19
S8	0723		
13X*	073	80	80

S4 Trailsite   0.1 m. E. of Trail at TM 0
S5 Spanish Lakes Trailsite at TM 0.3
S6 Spanish Lakes Trailsite at TM 0.4
S7 Spanish Lakes Trailsite at TM 0.8
S8 Beehive Lake   Trailsite at TM 1.5
  * 13X is point of intersection of trail 7 with trail 10 at Trail
  mile 6-3.5

Node	Segment	1	2
19			
14	074	309	86

No official campsites designated

Node	Segment	Reference Directional Transit Times in Minutes	
		1	2
10			
10.1	075	212	68
10.2	076	45	45
9	077	92	29

No official campsites designated

Node	Segment	1	2
6			
6.1	078	35	17
6.2	079	71	23
S9	080	7	7
S9	0813		
6.3	082	8	6
6.4	083	17	5
S10	084	32	19
S10	0353		
13X	086	12	7
6.5	087	12	7
7.0	088	26	7
S11	089	9	2
S11	0903		
7.1	091	25	30
7.1X	161	45	45
	162	13	15

Node	Segment	Reference Directional Transit Times in Minutes	
		1	2
HL3/HL3A			
HL3/HL3A	0923		
8.0	093	32	38
HL2	094	10	10
HL2	0953		
8.1	096	27	28
8.2/8X	097	111	31
8.3	099	40	69
8.4	100	37	21
HL5	101	000	0000
HL5	102.3		
9.0	103	45	45
9.1	104	24	86
9.2	105	39	44
1.0	106	97	109

S 9   Mirror Lake   Trailsite at TM 1.9
S10   Trailsite at TM 2.7 (Emerald Meadows?)
S11   Trailsite Summit Lake (small backpacking campsite)
HL3   Thompson Lake   0.1 m. E. of Trail at TM 5.1
HL3A Trailsite 0.1 m. W. of Trail at TM 5.1
HL2   0.4 m. S.E. of Trail at TM 6.4
HL5   Arrow Lake 0.1 m. S. of Trail at TM 10.8

Node	Segment	Reference Directional Transit Times in Minutes	
		1	2
11			
HL1	107	69	62
HL1	1083		
20	109	113	101
20.1	110	108	39
HL2	111	90	63
HL2	0953		
8.0	094	10	10

HL1   Trailsite 0.1 m. W. of Trail at TM 2.0
HL2   Trailsite at TM 8.9

Node	Segment	1	2
20			
21	114	128	107
21.1	115	132	48
HL4	116	0	0
HL4	1173		
21.2	118	72	36
21.3	119	14	51
21.4	120	26	7
7.0	121	666	8

HL4   Basin Gallatin Peak   0.4 m. N. of Trail at TM 6-5.6

Node	Segment	Reference Directional Transit Times in Minutes	
		1	2
5			
5.1	122	18	17
5.2	123	43	12
5.3	124	54	20
X.L	125	34	10
XL	1263		
8.2/8X			
	127	96	96
XL			

8X is the point of intersection of Trail from Diamond Lake to Indian Ridge 2.4 m. off Node 8

27			
	128	35	19
27.1			
	129	38	11
27.2			
	130	36	13
27.3			
	131	15	5
CS1			
	1323		
CS1			
	133	23	7
26			

CS1 Campsite 2.0 m. from Lava Lake Trail Head

Node	Segment	Reference Directional Transit Times in Minutes	
		1	2
26			
CS2	134	9	5
CS2	1353		
26.1	136	28	16
26.2	137	72	72
26.3	138	78	28
24	139	40	42
ZL	140	44	120
Z1	1413		
25	142	34	113

CS2   Campsite 2.5 m. from Lava Lake Trail Head

Node	Segment	1	2
23			
D1	143	108	39
D1	1443		
23.1	145	48	17
22	146	120	44
D6	048	50	20
	0493		

D1   Campsite 1.8 m. from Deer Lake Trail Head
D6   Campsite (Deer Lake) (.5 m. N. of node 22)

Node	Segment	Reference Directional Transit Times in Minutes	
		1	2
28			
21.3	147	216	162
24			
D4	148	38	32
D4	1493		
22	150	20	21
D3	151	10	5
D3	1523		
D7	153	40	21
D7	1543		
22.1	155	36	36
HL6	156	63	75
HL6	1573		
21	158	36	129

APPENDIX 3.B

Spanish Peaks Wilderness Compact Trail System

Node	Segment	Reference Directional Transit Times in Minutes	
		1	2
1			
	001	11	9
2			
	002	222	186
3			
	003	24	32
4			

No official campsites designated

3			
	004	188	112
C1			
	0053		
C1			
	006	35	20
17			

C1. Big Brother Lake 0.3 mile s. at TM3-4.25

17			
	007	88	156
18			
	0083		
18			
	009	91	157
4			

No official campsites designated

17			
	010	21	21
C2			
	0113		
C2			
	012	24	24
F4			
	0133		
F4			
	014	17	17
16			
	015	4	12
F5/F1			
	0163/0173		

Node	Segment	Reference Directional Transit Times in Minutes	
		1	2
F5/F1			
	018	24	24
F2			
	0193		
F2			
	020	43	91
TM 16-2.7			
	0213		
TM 16-2.7			
	022	34	67
S1			
	0233		
S1			
	024	3	5
5			
	025	3	3
S1'			
	0263		
S1'			
	027	65	72
2			

C2   Marcheta Lake   0.8 mi. S.W. of 17 at TM 0.6
F4   Jerome Rock Lakes   0.5 mi. S.W. of Trail at TM 1.3
F5   Lower Falls Creek Lake   0.25 mi. N.E. of 16 at TM 2.1
F2   Margo Lake   0.2 mi. S.E. of Trail at TM 2.8
S1   Trailside Campsite   0.1 mi. N.W. of Trail at 5.9, 6.1
S1'   Trailside Campsite   opposite S1, small, adjacent to Pioneer Falls

Node	Segment	1	2
16			
	014	17	17
F3/F4			
	0293/0133		
F3/F4			
	030	31	31
15			
	031	14	14
H3			
	0323		
H3			
	033	7	20
H2			
	0343		
H2			
	035	24	67

Node	Segment	Reference Directional Transit Times in Minutes	
		1	2
H1			
	0363		
H1			
	037	7	20
12			
	038	19	23
6			
	039	22	26
S2			
	0403		
S2			
	041	38	32
5			

F3	Jerome Rock Lakes	Trailside at TM 0.3
F4	Jerome Rock Lakes	Off trail S. 0.3 mi. at TM 0.3
F1	Upperfalls Creek L.	Off trail N. 0.3 mi. at TM 0.7
H2	Trailsite	Trailside at TM 2.0
H3	(Hermit Trail)	Off trail 0.5 mi. at TM 1.7
H1	Trailsite	Trailside at TM 2.7
H5	Hermit Lake	Off trail at TM 2.1
S2	Trailsite	0.2 mi. off trail at TM 4.3
5X	Pt. of Intersection	off trail 13 with trail 5 at 0.5 mi. S. of node 5

Node	Segment	1	2
15			
	031	14	14
H3			
	0323		
H3			
	042	7	7
H3'			
	0433		
H3'			
	044	14	14
H4			
	0453		
H4			
	046	7	7
14			
	047	47	47
13			
	048	0	0
S4			
	0493		

Node	Segment	Reference Directional Transit Times in Minutes	
		1	2
S4			
	050	20	40
S3			
	0513		
S3			
	052	33	65
12			
	038	19	23
6			

H3	Trailsite	0.2 mi. N.E. of Trail at TM 0.4
H3'	Trailsite	backpacking site at TM 0.6
H4	Trailsite	0.1 mi. N. of Trail at TM 0.8
S4	Trailsite	0.1 mi. E. of Trail at TM 2.2
H1	Trailsite	0.3 mi. W. of Trail at TM 4.3

Node	Segment		
13			
	048	0	0
S4			
	0493		
S4			
	053	14	8
S5			
	0543		
S5			
	055	5	3
S6			
	0563		
S6			
	057	19	11
S7			
	0583		
S7			
	059	34	19
S8			
	0603		
S8			
	061	80	80
13X			

S4	Trailsite	0.1 mi. E. of Trail at TM 0
S5	Spanish Lakes	Trailsite at TM 0.3
S6	Spanish Lakes	Trailsite at TM 0.4
S7	Spanish Lakes	Trailsite at TM 0.8
S8	Spanish Lakes	Trailsite at TM 1.5
13X	Pt. of intersection of trail 7 with Trail 10 at TM 6-3.5	

Node	Segment	Reference Directional Transit Times in Minutes	
		1	2
19	062	309	86
14			
No official campsites designated			
10	063	349	142
9			
No official campsites designated			
6	064	113	47
S9	0653		
S9	066	57	30
S10	067	12	7
13X	068	38	14
7	069	9	2
S11	0703		
S11	071	25	30
7.1			
7.1-7X	072	45	45
7.1	073	13	15
HL3/3A	0743		
HL3/3A	075	32	38
8	076	10	10
HL2	0773		
HL2	078	138	59

Node	Segment	Reference Directional Transit Times in Minutes	
		1	2
8.2/8X			
	079	77	90
HL5			
	6803		
HL5			
	081	45	45
9			
	082	160	239
1			

S9   Mirror Lake Trailsite at TM 1.9
S10 Trailsite at TM 2.7 (Emerald Meadows?)
S11 Trailsite Summit Lake (small backpacking campsite)
HL3 Thompson Lake 0.1 mi. E. of Trail at TM 5.1
HL3A Trailsite 0.1 mi. W. of Trail at TM 5.1
HL2 0.4 mi. S.E. of Trail at TM 6.4
HL5 Arrow Lake 0.1 mi. S. of Trail at TM 10.8

Node	Segment	1	2
11			
	083	69	62
HL1			
	0843		
HL1			
	085	113	101
20			
	0863		
20			
	087	198	102
HL2			
	0773		
HL2			
	076	10	10
8			

HL1 Trailside 0.1 mi. W. of Trail at TM 2.0
HL2 Trailsite at TM 8.9

Node	Segment	Reference Directional Transit Times in Minutes	
		1	2
20			
20	0863		
21	088	128	107
21	0893		
HL4	090	132	48
HL4	0913		
YL (21.3)	122	86	87
7	092	32	15

HL4   Basin Gallatin Peak   0.4 mi. N. of trail at TM 6-5.6 (?)

5	093	18	17
(5X)5.1	094	131	42
XL	0953		
XL			

8.2/8X	096	96	96
XL			

8X   is the point of intersection of Trail from Diamond Lake to Indian Ridge 2.4 mi. N.E. of node 8

27	097	124	48
CS1	0983		
CS1	099	23	7
26			

CS1   Campsite 2.0 mi. from Lava Lake Trail Head, Node 27

Node	Segment	Reference Directional Transit Times in Minutes	
		1	2
26			
	100	9	5
CS2			
	1013		
CS2			
	102	218	158
24			
	103	44	120
ZL			
	1043		
ZL			
	105	34	113
25			

CS2   Campsite 2.5 mi. from Lava Lake Trail Head, Node 27

23			
	106	108	39
D1			
	1073		
D1			
	108	168	61
22			
	109	50	20
D6			
	1103		
D6			

D1   Campsite   1.8 mi. from Deer Lake Trail Head, Node 23
D6   Campsite   (Deer Lake)   0.5 mi. N. of Node 22

28			
	111	216	162
YL/21.3			

Node	Segment	Reference Directional Transit Times in Minutes	
		1	2
24			
	112	38	32
D4			
	1133		
D4			
	114	20	21
22			
	115	10	5
D3			
	1163		
D3			
	117	40	21
D7			
	1183		
D7			
	119	99	111
HL6			
	1203		
HL6			
	121	36	129
21			

D3 Moon Lake Campsite 0.3 mi. W. of Node 22
D4 Table Mt. Trail Campsite 0.5 mi. E. of Node 22
D7 Upper Deer Creek Basin 1.0 mi. W. of Node 22
HL6 Hell Roaring Lake Campsite 11.0 mi. from Trail Head 11.

APPENDIX 3.C

Designation of Trails for Each Route
in Spanish Peaks Area

Route No.	Route Taken	Camp Sites	Nights
1	1 - 2 - 5 - 2 - 1	0	0
2	1 - 2 - S1 - 2 - 1	S1	2
3	1 - 2 - S1 - 2 - 1	S1	1
4	1 - 9 - HL5; HL5 - 8 - HL3; HL3 - 7 - S9; S9 - 6 - 5 - 2 - 1	HL5 HL3 S9	1 2 3
5	1 - 2 - 5 - 6 - S9; S9 - 7 - HL3; HL3 - 8 - HL5; HL5 - 9 - 1	S9 HL3 HL5	1 1 1
6	1 - 2 - 5 - 16 - F3 - 16 - 5 - 2 - 1	0	0
7	1 - 2 - 5 - F3; F3 - 5 - 2 - 1	F3	1
8	1 - 2 - 5 - 16 - F3; F3 - 16 - TM16-2.7; TM16-2.7 - 5 - 2 - 1	F3 TM16-2.7	1 1
9	1 - 2 - 5 - 16 - F3; F3 - 16 - 5 - 2 - 1	F3	2
10	1 - 2 - 5 - 6 - 12 - 15 - F3/4; F3/4 - 15 - 12 - 6 - 5 - 2 - 1	F3/4	2
11	1 - 2 - 5 - F2; F2 - 16 - F3/4; F3/4 - 16 - 5 - 2 - 1	F2 F3/4	1 1
12	1 - 2 - 5 - 16 - F4; F4 - 16 - 5 - 2 - 1	F4	3
13	1 - 2 - 5 - TM16-2.7 - 5 - 2 - 1	0	0
14	1 - 2 - 5 - TM16-2.7 - S1; S1 - 5 - 2 - 1	S1	1
15	1 - 2 - 5 - 16 - 15 - 12 - 6 - 5 - 2 - 1	0	0
16	1 - 2 - 5 - F1/5; F1/5 - 16 - 15 - 12 - 6 - 5 - 2-1	F1	1
17	1 - 2 - 5 - F1/5; F1/5 - 16 - 15 - 12 - 6 - 5 - 2-1	F1	3
18	1 - 2 - 5 - 16 - F4; F4 - 15 - 12 - S3; S3 - 13 - S7; S7 - 13 - 12 - 6 - 5 - 2 - 1	F4 S3 S7	2 1 3
19	1 - 2 - 5 - 16 - F4; F4 - 15 - 14 - 13 - S6; S6 - 13 - 12 - 6 - 5 - 2 - 1	F4 S6	2 2
20	1 - 2 - 5 - 16 - F4; F4 - 15 - 14 - 13 - S6; S6 - 13 - 12 - 6 - 5 - 2 - 1	F4 S6	3 3

Route No.	Route Taken	Camp Sites	Nights
21	1 - 2 - 5 - 16 - F4; F4 - 15 - 14 - 13 - S6; S6 - 13 - 12 - 6 - 5 - 2 - 1	F4 S6	1 1
22	1 - 2 - 5 - 6 - 5 - 2 - 1	0	0
23	1 - 2 - 5 - 6 - S9 - 6 - 12 - 13 - S6/7 - 13 - 12 - 6 - 5 - 2 - 1	0	0
24	1 - 2 - 5 - 6 - 12 - 13 - S6/7 - 13 - 12 - 6 - S9 - 6 - 5 - 2 - 1	0	0
25	1 - 2 - 5 - S2; S2 - 6 - S9; S9 - 6 - 12 - 13 - S6/7; S6/7 - 13 - 12 - 6 - 5 - 2 - 1	S2 S9 S6/7	1 1 1
26	1 - 2 - 5 - 6 - 12 - 15 - F4; F4 - 16 - 5 - 2 - 1	F4	1
27	1 - 2 - 3 - C1 - 3 - 2 - 1	0	0
28	1 - 2 - 3 - C1; C1 - 3 - 2 - 1	C1	2
29	1 - 2 - 3 - 17 - 16 - 5 - 2 - 1	0	0
30	1 - 2 - 3 - 17 - C2; C2 - 16 - 5 - 2 - 1	C2	2
31	1 - 2 - 5 - 6 - S9; S9 - 7 - HL3 - 7 - S9; S9 - 6 - 5 - 2 - 1	S9 S9	1 1
32	1 - 2 - 5 - 6 - 7 - 7.1X - 7TM1 - 7.1X - 7 - 6 - 5 - 2 - 1	0	0
33	1 - 2 - 5 - 6 - 7 - HL3; HL3 - 7 - 6 - 5 - 2 - 1	HL3	2
34	1 - 2 - 5 - 6 - 7 - HL3A; HL3A - 8 - 20 - 11	HL3A	1
35	1 - 2 - 5 - 6 - 7 - 8 - 20 - 11	0	0
36	1 - 2 - 5 - 6 - 7 - HL3; HL3 - 8 - 20 - HL1; HL1 - 11	HL3 HL1	1 1
37	1 - 2 - 5 - 6 - S9: S9 - 7 - HL3; HL3 - 8 - 20 - 11	S9 HL3	2 2
38	1 - 2 - 5 - 6 - 12 - 13 - 12 - 6 - 5 - 2 - 1	0	0
39	1 - 2 - 5 - 6 - 12 - 13 - S5; S5 - 13 - 12 - 6 - 5 - 2 - 1	S5	1
40	1 - 2 - 5 - 6 - 12 - 13 - S7; S7 - 13 - 12 - 6 - 5 - 2 - 1	S7	2
41	1 - 2 - 5 - 6 - 12 - 13 - S4; S4 - 13 - 12 - 6 - 5 - 2 - 1	S4	3

Route No.	Route Taken	Camp Sites	Nights
42	1 - 2 - 5 - 6 - 12 - 13 - S3; S3 - 13 - 12 - 6 - 5 - 2 - 1	S3	2
43	1 - 2 - 5 - 6 - 12 - 13 - S6; S6 - 13 - 12 - 6 - 5 - 2 - 1	S6	3
44	1 - 2 - 5 - 6 - 12 - 13 - S5; S5 - 13 - 12 - 6 - 5 - 2 - 1	S5	3
45	1 - 2 - 5 - 6 - 12 - 13 - S5; S5 - 13 - 12 - 6 - 5 - 2 - 1	S5	2
46	1 - 2 - 5 - 6 - 12 - 13 - S7; S7 - 13 - 12 - 6 - 5 - 2 - 1	S7	3
47	1 - 2 - 5 - 6 - 12 - 13 - S5; S5 - 13 - 12 - 6 - 5 - 2 - 1	S5	4
48	1 - 2 - 5 - 6 - 12 - 13 - S7; S7 - S8 - S7; S7 - 13 - 12 - 6 - 5 - 2 - 1	S7 S7	1 1
49	1 - 2 - 5 - 6 - S9 - 6 - 5 - 2 - 1	0	0
50	1 - 2 - 5 - 6 - S9; S9 - 6 - 5 - 2 - 1	S9	2
51	1 - 2 - 5 - 6 - S9; S9 - 6 - S2; S2 - 5 - 2 - 1	S9 S2	1 1
52	1 - 2 - 5 - XL - 5 - 2 - 1	0	0
53	1 - 2 - 5 - XL; XL - 5 - 2 - 1	XL	1
54	1 - 2 - 5 - XL; XL - 5 - 2 - 1	XL	4
55	1 - 2 - 5 - F2 - 5 - XL - 5 - 2 - 1	0	0
56	1 - 9 - 8 - HL3; HL3 - 8 - 9 - 1	HL3	1
57	1 - 9 - 8X - XL; XL - 5 - 2 - 1	XL	1
58	1 - 9 - 8X - XL - 5 - 2 - 1	0	0
59	1 - 2 - 5 - XL; XL - 5 - 6 - S9; S9 - 7 - 8 - HL2; HL2 - 20 - HL1; HL1 - 11	XL S9 HL2 HL1	1 1 1 1
60	1 - 9 - HL5 - 9 - 1 - 2 - 5 - TM16 - 27 - 5 - 2 - 1	0	0
61	1 - 2 - 5 - 16 - 17 - C1; C1 - 17 - 16 - 15 - 14 - 13 - S6; S6 - 13 - 12 - 6 - 5 - 2 - 1	C1 S6	2 6
62	1 - 2 - 5 - 6 - 12 - 15 - F1; F1 - 15 - 14 - 13 - S6; S6 - S8; S8 - S10 - 7 - HL3; HL3 - 8 - 9 - 1	F1 S6 S8 HL3	2 1 1 1

Route No.	Route Taken	Camp Sites	Nights
63	1 - 2 - 5 - 16 - F3; F3 - 15 - 14 - 15 - 16 - 17 - C1; C1 - 17 - 16 - 5 - 2 - 1	F3 C1	1 3
64	1 - 2 - 5 - 6 - 12 - 15 - 14 - 13 - 12 - 6 - 5 - 2 - 1	0	0
65	10 - 9 - HL5; HL5 - 8X - XL; XL - 8X - 8 - HL3A; HL3A - 7 - 8 - 20 - 11	HL5 XL HL3A	1 1 1
66	11 - 20 - 11	0	0
67	11 - 20 - 8 - 7 - HL3; HL3 - 8 - 20 - 11	HL3	1
68	11 - HL1; HL1 - 20 - 8 - HL3A; HL3A - 8 - 20 - HL1; HL1 - 11	HL1 HL3A HL1	1 2 1
69	11 - HL1; HL1 - 20 - 21 - 7 - HL3; HL3 - 8 - 20 - 11	HL1 HL3	1 1
70	11 - 20 - 8 - 7 - 13X - S8; S8 - 13X - 7 - 21 - 20 - 11	S8	3
71	11 - HL1; HL1 - 20 - HL2; HL2 - 8 - 7 - HL3A; HL3A - 8 - 20 - 11	HL1 HL2 HL3A	1 2 2
72	11 - 20 - 21; 21 - 20 - 11	21	2
73	11 - 20 - 21 - HL4; HL4 - 21 - 20 - 11	HL4	5
74	19 - 14 - 15 - 14 - 19	0	0
75	19 - 14 - H4; H4 - 14 - 19	H4	1
76	19 - 14 - 13 - S5; S5 - 13 - 14 - 19	S5	2
77	19 - 14 - 13 - S7; S7 - 13 - 14 - 19	S7	3
78	27 - 26 - 27	0	0
79	27 - 26 - CS2; CS2 - 26 - 27	CS2	1
80	27 - 26 - CS2; CS2 - 26 - 27	CS2	2
81	27 - 26 - CS2; CS2 - 26 - 27	CS2	3
82	27 - 26 - CS2; CS2 - 26 - 27	CS2	4
83	27 - 26 - CS2; CS2 - 26 - 27	CS2	5
84	27 - 26 - CS2; CS2 - 26 - 27	CS2	6
85	27 - 26 - CS2; CS2 - 24 - D4; D4 - 22 - 23	CS2 D4	1 1

Route No.	Route Taken	Camp Sites	Nights
86	27 - 26 - 24 - ZL; ZL - 25	ZL	1
87	25 - 24 - 25	0	0
88	23 - 22 - 23	0	0
89	23 - 22 - D6; D6 - 22 - 23	D6	1
90	23 - 22 - D6; D6 - 22 - 23	D6	2
91	23 - 22 - D6; D6 - 22 - 23	D6	3
92	23 - D1; D1 - 22 - D1; D1 - 22 - D1; D1 - 23	D1 D1 D1	1 1 1
93	28 - YL - 28	0	0
94	28 - 7 - S11; S11 - 8 - 8X - 9 - 1	S11	1
95	28 - 7 - 8 - HL3; HL3 - 8 - 7 - 28	HL3	2
96	11 - 20 - 21 - HL4; HL4 - YL - 28	HL4	1
97	10 - 9 - 8X - XL; XL - 5 - 2 - 1	XL	1
98	10 - 9 - HL5; HL5 - 8 - HL3; HL3 - 20; 20 - 21 - HL6; HL6 - 22 - 23	HL5 HL3 20 HL6	1 2 1 1
99	1 - 2 - 3 - 4 - 3 - 2 - 1	0	0
100	1 - 2 - 3 - 2 - 1	0	0
101	1 - 2 - 3 - 17 - 18; 18 - 4 - 3 - 2 - 1	18	1
102	1 - 2 - 5 - 16 - F4; F4 - 17 - 3 - 2 - 1	F4	1
103	1 - 2 - 5 - 16 - F3; F3 - 16 - 17 - C1; C1 - 17 - 16 - F5; F5 - 5 - 2 - 1	F3 C1 F5	1 2 3
104	1 - 2 - 5 - 16 - 15 - H4; H4 - 15 - 16 - 5 - 2 - 1	H4	3

APPENDIX 3.D

Probability of Route Selection

Route Number	Hiking Parties	Riding Parties
1	.050	.030
2	--	--
3	.006	--
4	.006	--
5	.002	--
6	.008	.030
7	--	.014
8	.002	--
9	.008	.014
10	--	.014
11	--	--
12	.002	--
13	.034	.014
14	--	--
15	--	--
16	.002	.014
17	.002	--
18	--	--
19	.002	--
20	.002	--
21	.006	--
22	.002	--
23	.006	--
24	--	--
25	--	.014
26	.002	.014
27	.002	--
28	--	.014
29	.006	.014
30	--	.030
31	.012	--
32	.002	--
33	--	.014
34	.006	--
35	--	.014
36	.002	--
37	.002	--
38	.016	.045
39	.002	.014
40	--	--
41	--	.045
42	--	.014
43	--	--
44	--	--
45	--	.014
46	--	--
47	.002	--
48	--	.014
49	.008	.014
50	.002	--

51	.002	--
52	.006	.014
53	.006	--
54	.002	--
55	--	--
56	.002	--
57	.002	--
58	.002	--
59	.002	--
60	--	--
61	--	--
62	.002	--
63	--	--
64	.002	--
65	.012	--
66	.034	--
67	.002	--
68	.002	--
69	.002	--
70	.002	--
71	.002	--
72	--	.014
73	.002	--
74	.012	--
75	.012	--
76	.024	--
77	.012	.072
78	.406	.086
79	.037	--
80	.012	--
81	.002	--
82	.002	--
83	.006	--
84	.002	--
85	.008	--
86	.006	--
87	.012	.072
88	.037	.072
89	.024	--
90	.024	--
91	.002	--
92	--	.072
93	--	.038
94	.012	--
95	.012	--
96	.012	.014
97	--	--
98	.012	--
99	--	.014
100	.008	--
101	--	.014
102	.002	--
103	.002	--
104	--	.014

CHAPTER 4

THE SPANISH PEAKS BASE CASE

4.1 EXPERIMENTAL DESIGN AND THE ROLE OF THE BASE CASE

A simulation model provides a numerical technique for performing experiments with mathematical or logical models, or both, that describe the activities of a real-world system. Naylor, Burdick, and Sasser (1969) have noted that in a computer simulation experiment with any model, attention must be given to four stages: (1) the development of a computer program for the model, (2) the validation of the model, (3) the experimental design, and (4) the analysis of simulated data. Clearly, these activities are not independent of one another. Chapter 2 has provided a heuristic description of the computer program developed for our simulation experiments.[1] In chapter 3 we have outlined the parameterization of the model for the Spanish Peaks Wilderness Area. Both field research and sample survey data have been utilized to construct the trail system, transit times, route definitions, and associated probability distributions. However, the use of such sample information does not constitute a validation of the model. There are two levels at which this validation must be addressed in order to determine whether or not the outputs of the simulation would compare with the actual outcomes of the process. Before discussing these problems it is desirable to review validation itself.

In most cases validation requires an examination of the outputs of the simulation model compared with those for the real-world system in order to assess the agreement between the two. It requires that there be established an acceptable level of confidence that inferences based on the model hold for the actual process as well. Naylor and Finger (1967) suggest three steps:

1. Formulate a set of hypotheses for the process.
2. Attempt to test these hypotheses and the assumptions of the model.
3. Compare the input–output transformations generated by the model with those of the real world.

[1] IBM-RFF *Wilderness Area Simulation Model User's Manual* (N.T.I.S. Accession No. PB 233 364/AS). More specific information on the structure of the program is available in section 4.3.

Many processes do not provide data that satisfy the assumptions of common statistical tests.[2] Van Horn (1969) suggests the following procedure[3]:

> Find people who are directly involved with the actual process. Ask them to compare actual with simulation output. To make the test a little more reputable, one might offer several sets of simulated data and see if "experienced" people can tell which is which. One might even test the classification for statistical significance. If people can discriminate, ask them how they do it. The experimenter can then decide if the detectable differences affect the inferences he wishes to make.

Validation of the simulation model as it is applied to the Spanish Peaks Wilderness Area must address two issues. (1) How accurate are the input data? That is, the results of the simulation model are a function of the defined trail system, route functions, transit times, arrival time scheduling, party mix, and the route assignment. Our specification of these input data is based on sample information and field tests, which implies that one must be concerned with the representativeness of the sample and with errors of measurement. A number of distributions have also been based on informed judgment. Inaccuracies in any one or all of these sources can distort the simulation model of the Spanish Peaks Area. (2) Is the process represented by the model an accurate description of the real-world activity? This question involves the behavioral assumptions which underlie the model itself and is independent of the data. However, the inappropriateness of a behavioral assumption may result in misinterpreting the sample information. That is, the data inputs are based on the requirements of the model. Inappropriate modeling of process can lead to distortions of the data so that they conform to the needs of the simulator.

Both of these questions are important and difficult to answer. We shall suggest that the validation of the model as a general description of wilderness behavior is essentially a question of how severely the model's output is affected by the rigid patterns we have had to impose on a party's behavior in the model. It is, therefore, a matter of degree. We recognize that in the real world many recreationists do not behave precisely as they are modeled; however, our concern is with a good approximation of aggregate behavior.

Validation for any particular area must address the issue of the "goodness of fit" between the model and the real-world behavior at that area. We shall suggest that wilderness recreation, by its very nature, makes field testing extremely expensive and largely impossible on the scale necessary to fully validate the model. A complete field test would require that

---

[2] Problems of autocorrelation are frequent in many simulation models dealing with time processes. See Naylor (1971).

[3] Van Horn (1969) pp. 241–242.

the manager have the ability to control use patterns in the area under study at a complete range of use levels. Moreover, it would be necessary to maintain complete records on the experiences of each user. There is also the further problem that each repetition of the real-world process is but one drawing from a process which has many stochastic components. Thus we would, in theory, desire to have a number of replications for each usage level. After all these data are assembled, they could then be compared with a similar array of outputs from the simulation model with conformable parameterizations. A comparison of the outputs of each process, i.e., the real world and the simulated, represents the only means of *complete* validation. Given the diverse character of most wilderness use, the data collection and monitoring of the area represent a problem of such dimensions as not to be feasible for any practical purpose.

Does all of this imply we cannot validate the model? We believe not, and propose the base case approach in conjunction with what Van Horn (1969) calls the Turing method. The base case approach calls for a parameterization of the model in conformity with a recreational period for some area which has been observed in the past. In our case it is for four weeks during the summer of 1970 in the Spanish Peaks Wilderness Area. We propose that those familiar with the area during this period can examine our output information from the simulation model and assess the validity of the model. Clearly, even if this test is passed satisfactorily, we must assume that the behavior patterns underlying our input data will not change dramatically over time if we are to use the model for the evaluation of managerial alternatives in this area in the future. It should be noted that this assumption does not preclude changes that do not affect the data input to our model. Moreover, it does not influence the validity of the model with the initial parameterization. Rather, these assumptions refer to the usefulness of the model as a tool for forecasting users' experiences in response to some managerial action which may take place at some time after the date of our data.

A second stage in the validation of the process described by the simulation model involves the definition and application of the model to additional base cases for other wilderness areas. If we assume reasonable homogeneity in the measurement errors that may be present in the data input across these areas and subject similarly defined base cases to scrutiny by those informed in the "outputs" of the respective real-world processes, then the sequential application of the so-called Turing tests will constitute further validation of the model itself.

The base case also plays an important role in our experimental design of the simulation runs with the model and in the analysis of the data. That is, the simulation experiments we have performed with the model yield multiple output measures which will be used to satisfy a variety of objectives. First, we shall consider variations from the base case to assess the quantitative significance of changes in the values of parameters which were postulated on the basis of informed judgment rather than sample information or field research. Second, we wish to determine the effects of alternative use intensities on the aggregate willingness-to-pay function for wilderness experiences in the area, based on the estimates of an individual relationship reported by Cicchetti and Smith (1973). The experiments will be used also to gauge the effect of managerial policies for the area at alternative use levels. Thus the estimation of a single response surface to describe the simulation model[4] is not adequate since a diverse set of objectives is involved. Accordingly, we have selected the base case as a frame of reference and will test the effects of variations in use patterns relative to the base case.

Finally, the stochastic nature of the process implies that the outputs of one replication of the model are analogous to drawing from a multivariate probability distribution. Our objective, as stated at the outset, was to estimate the expected or average experience a user might anticipate under alternative sets of conditions. Consequently, we must address the issue of measuring this central tendency. A single run of the model will not provide a reasonable estimate of this expected experience. This statement does not, of course, tell us how many runs will be sufficient. We shall address this issue later in the chapter and will utilize the base case parameterization to examine the effects of increased replications on our estimates of the experience that can be expected by any user.

The research strategy we have selected is one which has many objectives. The computational costs associated with large-scale experimentation have also served to limit the dimensionality of our tests. For the most part the tests will be one-factor tests. A large scale effort might have estimated a response surface for the model. However, such estimation requires that a fairly complete sampling of combinations of values for our distributions be selected so that the equation or equations used to represent the model are estimated over a sufficient segment of the design space. This analysis should be viewed as a first illustrative step in the investigation of the properties of the model.

The base case is defined by the transit times, route descriptions, and the route probability distributions given in chapter 3. As we noted at that point, there are 104 permissible routes which vary in length of time on the trail and in overall complexity. There are 79 trail segments and 34 campsites which comprise the system. During the four weeks of the base case run we have postulated that 240 parties will enter the area. Tables 4.1,

---

[4] In our case there are multiple response variables which are the joint outcomes of the process. Thus response surface modeling would have to take into account the interdependent character of the process which generates these outputs.

4.2, and 4.3 describe their season, days of the week, and hours within a day. The first two of these distributions are data based for the area, while the latter is based on informed judgment.

Tables 4.4 and 4.5 present the hiker-rider mix and the distribution of party sizes, given a mode of travel. These distributions together with the routes, transit times, time adjustment factor and the route probability distributions define the base case for the Spanish Peaks. There is, however, one further behavioral assumption in the model. This assumption relates to the allowed variation in transit time for each party and trail segment. In chapter 3 we described the specific manner in which the model arrives at transit times. For a given segment they are normally distributed, with a mean given by the transit time adjusted for the size and mode of travel of the party. The standard deviation has been set for each segment as a percent of the mean. For the base case, the ratio of standard deviation to mean was assumed to be 12 percent. Thus 95 percent of the parties' transit times will fall within ± 24 percent of the segment mean.

4.2 THE NEED FOR VARIANCE REDUCTION

As we have noted throughout chapters 2 and 3, the scheduling of parties over the simulated season time of each run, and the assignment of characteristics, including routes and transit times, are all the outcomes of probabilistic processes. Hence the measured outputs, i.e., encounters of different types, will be random variables and, therefore, given the same set of initial conditions over a number of experimental replications, we can expect variation in the recorded output variables. This problem can be easily illustrated with a comparison of a single run of the base case for the Spanish Peaks model versus the average of ten runs of the same base case. In the latter, we have maintained the same parameterization of the model. Thus, only the outcomes of the probabilistic decisions will vary from one run to the next.[5]

The simulation model provides a variety of summary tables for the results of each run.[6] We shall focus on four of these tables in the analysis of the remaining chapters. However, to illustrate their character for the Spanish Peaks case, we have selected seven of the tables, summarizing the results for the first run of the base case. In what follows we explain briefly the construction of each and their potential uses.

Table 4.6 presents the results of a single run for the complete system by party type. It records the total number of encounters of each type by

---

[5] Each replication must be an independent drawing from the population of outcomes the probabilistic process can provide.

[6] See *Wilderness Area Simulation Model User's Manual* for description of these outputs.

the relevant group. That is, the records of each party are summarized according to that party's size-mode of travel classification. Encounters are also recorded according to their classification when they occur on the trail and are simply designated total camp encounters for those in the camp-sites. Thus table 4.6 suggests that 60 medium-sized hiking parties used the area during the four-week period. As a group, they had 80 encounters with small hiking parties, 72 with medium, and so on. This would amount to an average of about 3.3 encounters (without regard to the size-mode of travel classification) per party encountered for the medium-sized hiking group. Similarly, the records for riders are for the group in each size category. We do not know the within-group variation in experience from these records. Several further points should be noted. This table is symmetrical in that the number of encounters small hiking parties had with medium riding parties must equal the number medium riding parties had with small hiking groups (i.e., 18).

It should also be noted that the sum of the column showing the number of parties is less than 240, which was designated as the total number of parties entering the area in the four weeks of the base case. The reason for the discrepancy (i.e., 225 versus 240) is that fifteen parties are still in the area at the end of the simulation period. Their routes call for their exit at some time after the end of the simulation period. This table summarizes the recorded encounters of those parties who have completed their trips.

Table 4.7 summarizes the same parties' records under an alternative dimension. Rather than aggregating by the size and mode of travel of each party, the data are summarized by the length of the trip (in days) which each party took during its stay in the area. The encounters are again summarized by the size and mode of travel of the parties encountered. This table indicates that the majority of the parties completing their trips (154 of 225) had one-day routes. Clearly, this group could not have camp encounters, since they did not stay overnight in the area. It should be noted that another variable describing camp encounters has also been included. Here the number of nights of at least one camp encounter for each party is also reported. In our summary, this variable provides the sum of these values across all parties with like trip lengths.

Tables 4.8 and 4.9 present these same aggregation schemes for a subset of all the encounters, namely, those which occurred on trail segments defined as the periphery of the area. The segments comprising our definition of the periphery are enumerated in appendix 4.A. The rationale for such disaggregation was noted in chapter 1. Different types of encounters under different conditions will affect the recreationist's utility functions in different ways. It has often been suggested that encounters at the trail head are less distasteful to the wilderness recreationist than those which occur in the interior of the area. The former are anticipated and consequently do not disrupt the perceived solitude of an individual's wilderness experience. While we do not have empirical evidence to provide hard and fast support for this hypothesis, there is a good reason to anticipate this differentiation according to the location of the encounter. It is interesting to note that the majority of the recorded encounters do occur on the so-called periphery segments. Assuming there is a significant difference in the measured effects of these encounters versus the effects of interior encounters on an individual's willingness to pay for wilderness experience, this information can be of value in developing managerial policies.

One further disaggregation in these data may also be useful. The trail encounters which a party has can occur in either of two ways, as we noted in chapter 2. The party can meet another party on a segment going in the opposite direction or it can overtake, or be overtaken by, another party going in the same direction. The time during which the other party or parties are perceived varies in each of these cases. With the meeting encounter, parties move away from each other at a rate which equals the sum of their individual speeds, while in the case of overtaking encounters, the rate is the difference in their respective velocities. It may be that the length of time a party perceives others in the immediate vicinity affects the severity of the effect for each of its members. This matter is clearly an empirical one that can be answered with data that can be collected. Nonetheless, the program allows the output by party type to be disaggregated according to the type of encounter (i.e., meeting versus overtaking). Tables 4.10 and 4.11 present these results for the base case. This run suggests that there were more meeting encounters than overtaking encounters during the four-week period. It should be noted that the number of parties is identical across the two tables, since these values of the encounters refer to the group as a whole (e.g., small hiking parties, medium riding parties, and so on).

The final table we shall present for this run of the Spanish Peaks base case is a partial sample of the summary by location of the encounters by trail and campsites. The complete table provides a complete record of those segments of the trail system or the campsites where the encounters we have noted occurred. Table 4.12 reports a selected sample of these results. It should be noted that the segments listed are *only* those which were utilized during the simulation run. That is, the table reports the trail segments which parties traversed or the campsites they used. It does not mean that encounters necessarily occurred on each segment. In fact, this run suggests that only a small subset of the trail segments experienced heavy encounters (i.e., 27, 97, and 99). An equally small number of campsites had the bulk of the encounters (i.e., 58, 74, 101, and 110).[7] If the results

[7] The trail segments and camps referred to here correspond numerically to the "compact" trail system of appendix 3.B.

of this run can be taken as representative (an issue which will be addressed directly), these data may help the manager decide where an investment in additional trail and/or campsite should be made or another management practice instituted.

As we have noted at the outset of this section, each recording for these encounter measures is a random variable. The intractable character of the process generating these random variables prevents us from furnishing an analytical description of their density functions. Clearly if such a description were available, there would be no need for a simulation model. Given the probabilistic nature of the process being simulated, it is necessary to provide some measures of the underlying probability distribution. A single replication of the model is one drawing from this underlying distribution and as such is not likely to tell us much of the character of the distribution. Consequently we have calculated the sample means and variances of each encounter measure in order to help describe their probability distributions.[8]

Tables 4.13 through 4.16 present the sample means and variances for ten independent replications of the base case. The first two of these tables conform in their respective mode of aggregation to tables 4.6 and 4.7 presented earlier. That is, they report encounters by party type and by trip length. The values in parentheses report the sample variances and the values above are the corresponding sample means. Several points should be noted. (1) The entries in the table are roughly comparable to those of the single replication. However, there is substantial variation in the measured encounters across replications of the same initial parameterization of the model. (2) The magnitude of the variance in measured encounters varies greatly across the designated control group and the category of the encounter parties. With trail encounters and hikers, the range in this variance is from a high of 339.8 to 0.7. These correspond to the variance in encounters of medium-sized hiking parties with other medium-sized hiking parties and the variance in recorded encounters of large hiking parties with large riding parties. The observed spread is not as great when riding parties are the control group. These differences in the magnitudes of the estimated variances imply that an increased number of replications will affect some of our outputs more than others. That is, our objective in increasing the replications of a given experiment is to reduce the variance in the output measure of interest. For our case it is the average number of

---

[8] There are, of course, other objective functions that might be considered in evaluating the performance of a managerial policy. One might consider minimizing the discrepancy between the worst and the best experiences of each group. Alternatively, a fixed threshold experience might be defined and we might want to minimize the number of individuals having experiences worse than the norm. Weighted objective functions in terms of the mean experience for a given group and the variance about the mean for that group may also be considered.

encounters in each category. Since the variances for these measures differ greatly from one category to the next, we cannot hope to obtain estimates for each encounter variable that are of consistent quality. (3) It would appear that the number of camp encounters exhibits the largest overall variation. This tendency is particularly true when the data are aggregated according to the trip length.

Tables 4.15 and 4.16 also report the averages and variance across ten replications for the encounters occurring on the periphery segments of the area. These tables can be compared with 4.8 and 4.9. The range of values for the variance in encounters across replications is somewhat larger when only the periphery is studied. The largest value for hiking parties is 402.4 and the smallest 0.8.

These findings are important because they affect our efforts at variance reduction. Simply stated, variance reduction refers to techniques which increase the efficiency with which a simulation model provides estimates of some unobservable parameter. There are a variety of techniques for accomplishing this objective, including repeated replications, antithetic variates, quasi-random numbers, and others (see Hammersley and Handscomb, 1964 and Newman and Odell, 1971 for a more detailed treatment). For our purposes, we wish to estimate the expected number of encounters and will assume existence of the first and second moments for each random variable (i.e., encounter measure). Consequently, we shall utilize the central limit theorem so that the variance in the mean encounters is $1/n$th (where n is the sample size), the variance in the original population. Clearly, the larger the sample size, the smaller the variability in the distribution of the sample means and hence the greater the focus in our inferential statements concerning encounters. However, the large differentials between the variation in one type of encounter versus another suggest that increasing the number of replications will not provide all estimates with the same level of precision. Moreover, if the focus of attention were on one kind of encounter, say camp encounters by those with two-day trips versus the trail encounters with riding parties of the same group, it may be that a different number of replications would be indicated.

The purpose of this research is to (1) illustrate how the model might be applied to a reasonably large wilderness area; (2) examine the sensitivity of the model's results to certain parameter changes; and (3) illustrate how the results of the simulator might be linked with estimated relationships describing the effect of encounters on willingness to pay for use of the same area. Thus it is not possible to isolate one or more encounter measures as the focus of attention. Rather, all the outputs of the model are important. In the next section we discuss the effects of increased replications on our estimates of the various encounter measures.

4.3   THE EFFECT OF THE NUMBER OF REPLICATIONS

It should be noted at the outset that every increase in the number of replications of a given experiment will serve to reduce the variance in the sample mean. Thus in the absence of other constraints, the larger the number of replications, the better. There is, however, an important constraint in simulating events with a model of this size, i.e., the cost of experimentation. The costs associated with ten replications of the base case of the Spanish Peaks model on an IBM 370-155 are approximately $150. The cost associated with doubling or tripling the number of replications is somewhat less than two and three times this figure if the runs can be made under one compilation of the program. GPSS V provides the option of multiple runs of any given scenario through the use of the CLEAR option. However, even with the use of this procedure to save on assembly time, the program for an area of this size requires fairly extensive computational resources.[9] In addition to the costs associated with the computer time for simulations with the model, there are additional costs which must be incurred in summarizing the outputs from the model. In its present form the model does not calculate the summary statistics across the replications of a single experiment. While the program can be modified in the future to permit such calculations, it has not been modified to date. Thus the outputs must be transcribed from the simulation outputs to machine-readable form and supplemental FORTRAN programs applied to these data to yield the summary statistics. The costs associated with these functions are also significant.

Given a modest computer budget, we have decided to illustrate the effects of increased replications by comparing the results for the base case under ten, twenty, and thirty replications. As we noted earlier in this chapter, our attention will focus on four tables—encounters by party type, by trip length, by party type on the periphery, and by trip length on the periphery. Given the wide array of output options, four tables may seem to be but a small sample of the outputs. This sample does, however, involve summary statistics for 166 random variables. Tables 4.17 and 4.18 present the means and variances for the encounter measures when aggregated by party type with twenty and thirty replications, respectively. The estimated variances across replications for each variable are for the most part comparable to the values reported under ten replications in table 4.13. Hence increasing the replications to twenty and thirty can be said to in-

---

[9] The costs associated with running the model are determined by: (1) the size of the model in terms of the number of trail segments and campsite; (2) the length of the simulated season; and (3) the number of parties using the area. Costs range from $150 to $300 for ten replications with a four-week run of the Spanish Peaks model.

crease the efficiency (as measured by the variance) in the estimates of the expected value by approximately two and three times, respectively. There are one or two rather glaring exceptions. The variance in encounters by small hikers with other small hikers has increased by a factor of five to six over that observed with ten replications. Casual observation might suggest that this increase is indicative of a nonfinite second moment.

The prospect of one or more of the encounter variables following a probability distribution without finite moments can have serious implications for our characterization of what degree of disruption any individual can expect during a particular trip. Simply stated, our sample moments (e.g., mean) would not provide good estimates of the central tendencies of the probability distributions involved. However, it appears that this problem is unlikely, since the estimated variance for this variable with thirty replications is less than that for twenty.[10] The remaining tables are available in appendix 4.A.

Table 4.19 reports the average (across replications) number of encounters by party type for each of the three replication levels. It clearly indicates that the average number of encounters in each category is remarkably stable with increases in the sample size. This observation holds for nearly all categories of encounters. The greatest percentage differential between the highest and lowest estimate is approximately 80 percent for encounters that medium riding parties experienced with large riding parties. For the most part, all estimates are within 10 percent of each other. On the basis of this stability in our estimates of the expected number of encounters and consideration of the computational costs, we have selected ten replications as sufficient for the experiments that follow in the next chapter.

4.4 SUMMARY

This chapter has addressed three issues—model validation, the role of our base case, and variance reduction. Each of these areas is important to any simulation exercise. Since the operational significance of a simulation model is largely a function of its ability to portray real-world processes, the question of model validation is of considerable importance. We have noted that if all the information necessary for complete validation of the model were available, it is not clear that a simulation model would need to have been constructed. Thus we must be satisfied with a less than complete validation of the wilderness users' travel behavior simulator. With the present paucity of data and difficulty in performing controlled experiments, we have chosen the Turing method. This amounts to allowing the model's outputs to be reviewed by experienced wilderness managers

[10] See Smith (1975) for a discussion of tests for detecting infinite variance distributions.

(i.e., those familiar with use patterns at the Spanish Peaks Wilderness Area) and letting them judge whether it provides a reasonable description. In order to facilitate such a general review, we have defined a base case for the area. That is, the model has been parameterized using sample information on users and use patterns in the summer of 1970. The outputs for this base case are reported in this chapter and the model's results in the chapters which follow may be evaluated with reference to this base case.

In addition we have suggested that the definition of similar base cases for other areas is useful before we claim that the model is generally applicable to all wilderness recreation. One of the primary purposes of this study is to illustrate the use of the model so that further validation might proceed. The base case also functions as a frame of reference for the further experiments to be performed with the model. It seeks to represent 1970 use patterns so that changes in the level of use might be construed as the result of managerial prerogative or exogenous growth patterns.

Since the measured outputs of the model are random variables, some attention had to be directed to the means selected for estimating the expected number of encounters. A single simulation represents a single drawing from the probabilistic process. Multiple runs are necessary if we are to discern a central tendency and variability about it. It should be clear that in principle a larger number of replications is better than any smaller number in the absence of additional constraints. However, computational costs with a large-scale model prohibit a large number of replications of each experiment from being undertaken. An examination of the average number of encounters for runs of ten, twenty, and thirty replications suggests little variation in these means and reasonable stability in the estimated variances. Hence, given the testing and analysis which will follow, and cost considerations, we have selected ten replications of each experiment as a sufficient level of variance reduction.

REFERENCES

Cicchetti, C. J., and V. K. Smith. 1973. "Congestion, Quality Deterioration, and Optimal Use: Wilderness Recreation in the Spanish Peaks Primitive Area," *Social Science Research,* vol. 2 (March).

Hammersley, J. M., and D. C. Handscomb. 1964. *Monte Carlo Methods* (New York: John Wiley & Sons).

Handscomb, D. C. 1969. "Monte Carlo Techniques: Theoretical" in *The Design of Computer Simulation Experiments,* edited by T. H. Naylor (Durham, N.C.: Duke University Press).

Naylor, T. H. 1971. *Computer Simulation Experiments with Models of Economic Systems* (New York: John Wiley & Sons).

————, D. S. Burdick, and W. E. Sasser, Jr. 1969. "The Design of Computer Simulation Experiments," in *The Design of Computer Simulation Experiments,* edited by T. H. Naylor (Durham, N.C.: Duke University Press).

————, and J. M. Finger. 1967. "Verification of Computer Simulation Models," *Management Science* (October).

Newman, T. G., and D. L. Odell. 1971. *The Generation of Random Variates* (New York: Hafner Publishing).

Smith, V. K. 1975. "A Simulation Analysis of the Power of Several Tests for Detecting Heavy-Tailed Distributions," *Journal of the American Statistical Association* (September).

Van Horn, Richard. 1969. "Validation," in *The Design of Computer Simulation Experiments,* edited by T. H. Naylor (Durham, N.C.: Duke University Press).

TABLE 4.1.   Weekly Distribution of Use

Week Number	Percent of Total Parties Entering
1	10
2	30
3	30
4	30

TABLE 4.2.   Daily Distribution of Use

Day of the Week	Percent of Parties Entering in the Week
Monday	11
Tuesday	6
Wednesday	7
Thursday	8
Friday	16
Saturday	30
Sunday	22

TABLE 4.3.   Hourly Distribution of Use

Time Interval	Percent of Parties in Given Day
7:30 - 9:00 a.m.	26
9:00 - 10:30 a.m.	28
10:30 - 12:00 noon	26
12:00 - 1:30 p.m.	16
1:30 - 3:00 p.m.	3
3:00 - 4:30 p.m.	1

TABLE 4.4. Hiker-Rider Mix

Party's Mode of Travel	Percent of Total Parties
Hiking	75
Horseback	25

TABLE 4.5. Size Distribution of Parties

Size of Party	Percent of Party Type	
	Hiking	Horseback
Small	50	46
Medium	34	39
Large	16	15

TABLE 4.6. Spanish Peaks Base Case — Encounters by Party Type

Party Type	Number of Parties	Trail Encounters						Camp Encounters
		Hikers			Riders			
		Small	Medium	Large	Small	Medium	Large	
Hikers								
Small	90	90	80	23	10	18	10	31
Medium	60	80	72	18	11	13	4	14
Large	27	23	18	12	4	4	1	15
Riders								
Small	22	10	11	4	2	1	1	7
Medium	20	18	13	4	1	6	2	7
Large	6	10	4	1	1	2	4	6

TABLE 4.7. Spanish Peaks Base Case — Encounters by Trip Length

Days on Trip	Number of Parties	Trail Encounters						Camp Encounters	
		Hikers			Riders			Number	Nights
		Small	Medium	Large	Small	Medium	Large		
1	154	176	166	47	24	30	8	0	0
2	21	13	9	5	1	3	3	11	10
3	27	19	16	4	2	7	2	21	16
4	17	17	4	4	2	3	8	39	27
5	3	4	1	0	0	0	0	5	4
6	2	2	2	2	0	1	1	3	2
7	1	0	0	0	0	0	0	1	1

TABLE 4.8. Spanish Peaks Base Case — Encounters on the Periphery by Party Type

Party Type	Number of Parties	Trail Encounters						Camp Encounters
		Hikers			Riders			
		Small	Medium	Large	Small	Medium	Large	
Hikers								
Small	84	88	78	21	9	18	10	0
Medium	59	78	68	17	10	13	4	0
Large	23	21	17	12	3	3	1	0
Riders								
Small	19	9	10	3	2	1	1	0
Medium	19	18	13	3	1	6	1	0
Large	6	10	4	1	1	1	4	0

TABLE 4.9.   Spanish Peaks Base Case — Encounters on the Periphery by Trip Length

Days on Trip	Number of Parties	Trail Encounters						Camp Encounters	
		Hikers			Riders			Number	Nights
		Small	Medium	Large	Small	Medium	Large		
1	152	174	165	47	22	29	8	0	0
2	21	13	9	4	1	3	3	0	0
3	22	17	13	3	1	7	2	0	0
4	9	14	2	2	2	2	7	0	0
5	3	4	0	0	0	0	0	0	0
6	2	2	1	1	0	1	1	0	0
7	1	0	0	0	0	0	0	0	0

TABLE 4.10. Spanish Peaks Base Case — Meeting Encounters by Party Type

	Number of Parties	Trail Encounters					
		Hikers			Riders		
		Small	Medium	Large	Small	Medium	Large
Hiker							
Small	90	88	73	21	9	17	10
Medium	60	73	66	18	8	11	4
Large	27	21	18	12	3	4	1
Rider							
Small	22	9	8	3	2	1	0
Medium	20	17	11	4	1	4	2
Large	6	10	4	1	0	2	4

TABLE 4.11. Spanish Peaks Base Case — Overtaking Encounters by Party Type

	Number of Parties	Trail Encounters					
		Hikers			Riders		
		Small	Medium	Large	Small	Medium	Large
Hiker							
Small	90	2	7	2	1	1	0
Medium	60	7	6	0	3	2	0
Large	27	2	0	0	1	0	0
Rider							
Small	22	1	3	1	0	0	1
Medium	20	1	2	0	0	2	0
Large	6	0	0	0	1	0	0

TABLE 4.12. Spanish Peaks Base Case — Encounters by Location

Trail Segment or Campsite[a]	Trail Encounters						Camp Encounters	
	Hikers			Riders				
	Small	Medium	Large	Small	Medium	Large	Camp	Nights
1	2	8	0	0	2	0	0	0
2	0	0	0	0	0	0	0	0
27	19	27	3	2	10	1	0	0
583	0	0	0	0	0	0	26	15
743	0	0	0	0	0	0	16	13
97	132	108	38	15	5	8	0	0
99	27	16	5	2	0	0	0	0
1013	0	0	0	0	0	0	10	7
1103	0	0	0	0	0	0	16	13

TABLE 4.13. Spanish Peaks Base Case — Encounters by Party Type, Ten Replications

Party Type	Number of Parties	Trail Encounters Hikers Small	Medium	Large	Riders Small	Medium	Large	Camp Encounters
Hikers								
Small	84.9 (24.11)	108.0 (153.6)	76.1 (124.9)	30.9 (99.1)	15.6 (25.2)	12.1 (18.3)	5.7 (7.4)	44.8 (106.0)
Medium	60.5 (23.7)	76.1 (124.9)	63.5 (339.8)	25.0 (81.4)	10.6 (30.4)	10.1 (22.7)	3.4 (7.0)	23.6 (105.2)
Large	28.4 (11.2)	30.9 (99.1)	25.0 (81.4)	11.0 (20.2)	7.4 (23.8)	3.9 (4.1)	1.1 (0.7)	12.7 (21.2)
Riders								
Small	24.5 (18.7)	15.6 (25.2)	10.6 (30.4)	7.4 (23.8)	4.0 (6.4)	3.4 (10.6)	2.7 (4.0)	15.6 (273.0)
Medium	21.1 (11.7)	12.1 (18.3)	9.8 (24.2)	6.2 (43.0)	3.4 (10.6)	4.2 (14.0)	1.5 (0.9)	10.3 (58.6)
Large	7.3 (4.6)	5.7 (7.4)	3.4 (7.0)	1.1 (0.7)	3.0 (5.0)	1.5 (0.9)	1.0 (1.8)	4.0 (12.8)

Note: The values reported in this table are the estimated arithmetic means of the relevant variables across ten independent replications of the base case scenario. In parentheses below each item in the table is the estimated variance across the replications.

TABLE 4.14. Spanish Peaks Base Case — Encounters by Trip Length, Ten Replications

Party Type	Number of Parties	Trail Encounters						Camp Encounters
		Hikers			Riders			
		Small	Medium	Large	Small	Medium	Large	
Hikers								
Small	149.2 (36.8)	184.2 (365.2)	145.21 (1050.2)	59.6 (293.2)	20.8 (50.8)	19.5 (80.7)	6.3 (4.4)	0.0 (0.0)
Medium	27.8 (20.6)	24.4 (74.2)	17.6 (30.8)	7.1 (19.5)	6.7 (10.2)	4.8 (7.0)	2.9 (5.1)	10.1 (9.7)
Large	24.8 (14.4)	19.3 (19.0)	14.7 (21.6)	5.9 (14.1)	10.1 (33.1)	5.7 (4.8)	2.4 (3.4)	22.3 (26.4)
Riders								
Small	16.8 (34.6)	12.0 (27.8)	6.0 (10.6)	4.6 (11.0)	4.1 (17.9)	2.8 (9.0)	2.5 (7.1)	26.1 (188.1)
Medium	4.1 (1.9)	3.4 (1.6)	1.8 (1.0)	0.8 (0.8)	1.3 (1.0)	0.9 (1.9)	0.6 (0.8)	5.1 (8.1)
Large	1.4 (1.4)	1.6 (1.8)	1.1 (1.7)	0.7 (0.6)	0.1 (0.1)	0.1 (0.1)	0.1 (0.1)	2.4 (6.4)
	2.6 (1.2)	3.5 (28.7)	2.1 (5.5)	0.6 (0.6)	0.9 (1.1)	1.1 (1.7)	0.6 (0.8)	5.4 (26.8)

Note: The values reported in this table are the estimated arithmetic means of the relevant variables across ten independent replications of the base case scenario. In parentheses below each item in the table is the estimated variance across the replications.

TABLE 4.15.   Spanish Peaks Base Case — Encounters on the Periphery by Party Type, Ten Replications

Party Type	Number of Parties	Trail Encounters					
		Hikers			Riders		
		Small	Medium	Large	Small	Medium	Large
Hiker							
Small	79.6 (23.0)	101.2 (113.8)	72.9 (128.3)	29.8 (98.6)	14.0 (25.6)	10.8 (17.0)	5.4 (7.4)
Medium	57.9 (23.9)	72.9 (128.3)	10.3 (402.4)	23.4 (90.2)	9.4 (28.2)	9.4 (23.8)	3.2 (7.2)
Large	26.6 (9.0)	29.8 (98.6)	23.4 (90.2)	10.4 (15.8)	6.7 (20.6)	3.1 (3.3)	1.0 (0.8)
Rider							
Small	22.5 (17.3)	14.0 (25.6)	9.4 (28.2)	6.7 (20.6)	3.2 (5.0)	2.7 (6.4)	2.6 (4.2)
Medium	19.8 (14.2)	10.5 (20.7)	9.4 (23.8)	3.1 (3.3)	2.7 (6.4)	3.8 (13.2)	1.2 (0.8)
Large	7.0 (4.0)	6.0 (16.2)	3.2 (7.2)	1.0 (0.8)	2.6 (4.2)	1.2 (0.8)	1.0 (1.8)

Note: The values reported in this table are the estimated arithmetic means of the relevant variables across ten independent replications of the base case scenario. In parentheses below each item in the table is the estimated variance across the replications.

TABLE 4.16. Spanish Peaks Base Case — Encounters on the Periphery by Trip Length, Ten Replications

Days on Trip	Number of Parties	Trail Encounters					
		Hikers			Riders		
		Small	Medium	Large	Small	Medium	Large
1	147.3 (35.6)	181.1 (386.7)	142.6 (1067.6)	58.1 (292.1)	18.9 (34.3)	18.1 (83.3)	6.0 (4.4)
2	25.8 (12.8)	21.9 (72.7)	15.6 (26.8)	6.4 (16.2)	6.1 (12.5)	4.0 (3.8)	2.8 (5.6)
3	21.4 (5.2)	14.5 (10.7)	11.8 (16.4)	4.4 (6.2)	8.8 (21.4)	5.1 (5.3)	2.2 (3.2)
4	10.8 (15.2)	9.3 (24.6)	4.5 (6.3)	3.7 (8.4)	2.9 (7.7)	1.9 (4.7)	2.2 (6.4)
5	4.1 (1.9)	2.6 (1.8)	1.5 (0.9)	0.7 (0.8)	1.1 (0.7)	0.8 (1.6)	0.5 (0.5)
6	1.4 (1.4)	1.3 (1.4)	0.8 (1.0)	0.6 (0.4)	0.1 (0.1)	0.1 (0.1)	0.1 (0.1)
7	2.6 (1.2)	2.8 (18.0)	1.9 (4.3)	0.5 (0.5)	0.7 (0.6)	0.7 (1.4)	0.6 (0.8)

Note: The values reported in this table are the estimated aritithmetic means of the relevant variables across ten independent replications of the base case scenario. In parentheses below each item in the table is the estimated variance across the replications.

TABLE 4.17.   Spanish Peaks Base Case — Encounters by Party Type, Twenty Replications

Party Type	Number of Parties	Trail Encounters						Camp Encounters
		Hikers			Riders			
		Small	Medium	Large	Small	Medium	Large	
Hikers								
Small	85.6 (87.0)	100.3 (1077.7)	72.5 (175.6)	33.5 (104.5)	16.2 (41.7)	12.4 (21.0)	6.1 (13.0)	37.3 (247.4)
Medium	59.8 (47.0)	72.5 (175.6)	49.6 (572.2)	24.6 (47.0)	12.9 (38.7)	9.9 (15.5)	2.7 (5.6)	24.8 (115.2)
Large	27.8 (27.5)	33.5 (104.5)	24.6 (47.0)	11.8 (38.0)	7.6 (10.3)	5.1 (7.6)	1.9 (1.8)	12.6 (44.5)
Riders								
Small	27.2 (14.6)	16.2 (41.7)	12.9 (38.7)	7.6 (10.3)	7.7 (19.3)	6.3 (10.9)	2.5 (3.0)	12.0 (36.9)
Medium	21.0 (10.7)	12.4 (21.0)	9.9 (15.5)	5.1 (7.6)	6.8 (16.4)	4.6 (12.8)	2.8 (7.0)	10.8 (40.7)
Large	8.0 (7.6)	6.1 (13.0)	2.7 (5.6)	2.1 (2.6)	2.3 (2.4)	2.8 (7.0)	0.9 (2.2)	3.7 (15.5)

Note: The values reported in this table are the estimated arithmetic means of the relevant variables across ten independent replications of the base case scenario. In parentheses below each item in the table is the estimated variance across the replications.

TABLE 4.18. Spanish Peaks Base Case — Encounters by Party Type, Thirty Replications

Party Type	Number of Parties	Trail Encounters						Camp Encounters
		Hikers			Riders			
		Small	Medium	Large	Small	Medium	Large	
Hikers								
Small	85.1 (45.4)	99.9 (759.6)	71.7 (148.0)	35.2 (120.1)	17.3 (46.7)	13.9 (45.7)	5.5 (12.4)	31.9 (298.9)
Medium	59.6 (39.3)	71.7 (148.0)	48.6 (316.0)	24.1 (65.2)	14.1 (35.0)	10.6 (17.7)	4.1 (4.6)	24.4 (193.7)
Large	26.3 (17.7)	35.2 (120.1)	24.1 (65.2)	11.0 (26.6)	5.4 (7.5)	5.2 (3.4)	1.4 (2.1)	8.7 (20.3)
Riders								
Small	25.5 (16.1)	17.3 (46.7)	14.1 (35.0)	5.4 (7.5)	6.9 (23.1)	5.0 (8.2)	2.5 (4.4)	12.7 (74.3)
Medium	21.6 (12.9)	13.9 (45.7)	10.6 (17.7)	5.2 (3.4)	5.0 (8.2)	5.9 (19.1)	2.2 (2.4)	9.6 (47.7)
Large	8.4 (6.8)	5.5 (12.4)	4.1 (4.6)	1.4 (2.1)	2.5 (4.4)	2.2 (2.4)	0.5 (1.0)	4.3 (22.4)

Note: The values reported in this table are the estimated arithmetic means of the relevant variables across ten independent replications of the base case scenario. In parentheses below each item in the table is the estimated variance across the replications.

TABLE 4.19.   The Effects of Replications on the Estimate of Expected Encounters

Type of Trail Encounter	Number of Replications		
	10	20	30
Small H P [a] with:			
Small H P	108.0	100.3	99.9
Medium H P	76.1	72.5	71.7
Large H P	30.9	33.5	35.2
Small R P	15.6	16.2	17.3
Medium R P	12.1	12.4	13.9
Large R P	5.7	6.1	5.5
Medium H P with:			
Medium H P	63.5	49.6	48.6
Large H P	25.0	24.6	24.1
Small R P	10.6	12.9	14.1
Medium R P	10.1	9.9	10.6
Large R P	3.4	2.7	4.1
Large H P with:			
Large H P	11.0	11.8	11.0
Small R P	7.4	7.6	5.4
Medium R P	3.9	5.1	5.2
Large R P	1.1	1.9	1.4
Small R P with:			
Small R P	4.0	7.7	6.9
Medium R P	3.4	6.3	5.0
Large R P	2.7	2.5	2.5
Medium R P with:			
Medium R P	4.2	4.6	5.9
Large R P	1.5	2.8	2.2
Large R P with:			
Large R P	1.0	0.9	0.5

[a]H P designates Hiking Parties and R P designates Riding Parties.

APPENDIX 4.A

Periphery Trail Segments

Trail Segment Number	*Trail Segment Number*
1	97
2	99
22	100
27	103
39	105
41	106
63	108
83	109
85	111

APPENDIX 4.B

Estimated Expected Encounters and Variances for the Base Case

The tables that follow in this appendix present the results for twenty and thirty replications of the base case when encounters are aggregated by trip length and for encounters on the periphery aggregated according to both party type and trip length. The values in each table are the arithmetic means and the variances estimated across the replications of the base case experiment.

TABLE 4.B.1. Spanish Peaks Base Encounters by Trip Length, Twenty Replications

Days on Trip	Number of Parties	Trail Encounters						Camp Encounters	
		Hikers			Riders			Number	Nights
		Small	Medium	Large	Small	Medium	Large		
1	153.8 (66.3)	184.4 (1450.5)	130.3 (1070.2)	64.7 (355.5)	27.8 (94.1)	20.9 (68.5)	8.3 (25.3)	0.0 (0.0)	0.0 (0.0)
2	24.3 (13.8)	18.4 (33.0)	14.1 (15.7)	6.6 (8.2)	6.1 (7.3)	5.9 (10.0)	2.7 (3.0)	13.3 (38.2)	8.3 (12.0)
3	26.7 (19.8)	20.0 (44.0)	15.4 (26.5)	5.9 (6.0)	10.3 (21.9)	7.1 (8.0)	3.5 (5.1)	36.2 (170.7)	23.8 (44.7)
4	18.3 (22.0)	12.4 (24.2)	8.3 (10.8)	5.2 (11.2)	6.7 (19.0)	5.5 (9.2)	2.0 (3.6)	36.3 (273.4)	25.7 (123.6)
5	3.2 (3.0)	2.3 (3.4)	1.9 (4.2)	1.0 (1.3)	1.3 (1.3)	0.9 (1.6)	0.2 (0.3)	8.8 (65.9)	5.7 (19.1)
6	1.8 (1.8)	2.3 (8.8)	1.5 (3.7)	0.7 (0.7)	0.3 (0.2)	0.2 (0.2)	0.0 (0.0)	3.8 (11.5)	2.8 (7.9)
7	1.1 (1.3)	1.2 (2.5)	0.8 (2.3)	0.4 (0.3)	0.7 (1.4)	0.6 (0.5)	0.2 (0.2)	2.9 (26.3)	2.2 (13.7)

Note: The values reported in this table are the estimated arithmetic means of the relevant variables across twenty independent replications of the base case scenario. In parentheses below each item in the table is the estimated variance across the replications.

TABLE 4.B.2. Spanish Peaks Base Encounters on the Periphery by Party Type, Twenty Replications

| Party Type | Number of Parties | Trail Encounters | | | | | | Camp Encounters |
| | | Hikers | | | Riders | | | |
		Small	Medium	Large	Small	Medium	Large	
Hikers								
Small	81.0 (96.9)	95.6 (1161.0)	69.2 (182.8)	32.4 (104.6)	14.7 (34.5)	11.0 (21.5)	5.0 (11.0)	
Medium	56.4 (45.9)	69.2 (182.8)	47.1 (531.0)	23.6 (53.9)	11.9 (31.9)	8.8 (16.8)	2.5 (4.7)	
Large	25.6 (20.6)	32.4 (104.6)	23.6 (53.9)	11.2 (35.0)	7.1 (8.9)	4.6 (7.0)	1.8 (1.8)	
Riders								
Small	25.4 (15.3)	14.7 (34.5)	11.9 (31.9)	7.1 (8.9)	6.4 (14.2)	5.6 (10.5)	2.0 (2.1)	
Medium	19.5 (11.1)	11.0 (21.5)	8.8 (16.8)	4.6 (7.0)	5.6 (10.5)	3.7 (8.1)	2.5 (5.8)	
Large	7.9 (7.5)	5.5 (11.0)	2.5 (4.7)	1.8 (1.8)	2.0 (2.1)	2.5 (5.8)	0.8 (1.8)	

Note: The values reported in this table are the estimated arithmetic means of the relevant variables across twenty independent replications of the base case scenario. In parentheses below each item in the table is the estimated variance across the replications.

TABLE 4.B.3.   Spanish Peaks   Base Case Encounters on the Periphery by Length of Trip, Twenty Replications

Days on Trip	Number of Parties	Trail Encounters					
		Hikers			Riders		
		Small	Medium	Large	Small	Medium	Large
1	151.2 (69.8)	181.3 (1481.3)	128.1 (1055.2)	63.7 (350.4)	25.6 (84.0)	19.2 (59.6)	7.7 (24.4)
2	22.7 (9.4)	16.7 (24.6)	12.6 (16.9)	6.0 (7.3)	5.5 (5.6)	5.3 (8.8)	2.4 (2.7)
3	22.8 (16.5)	16.2 (22.0)	12.7 (19.6)	5.1 (3.7)	8.9 (18.9)	6.0 (7.6)	3.1 (3.4)
4	13.2 (11.7)	9.3 (17.1)	6.7 (10.8)	4.3 (8.7)	5.8 (14.5)	4.2 (5.4)	1.7 (2.1)
5	3.2 (3.0)	2.0 (3.0)	1.3 (3.5)	0.7 (0.7)	1.1 (1.5)	0.8 (1.4)	0.2 (0.3)
6	1.8 (1.8)	1.9 (6.6)	1.3 (3.0)	0.6 (0.7)	0.3 (0.2)	0.2 (0.2)	0.0 (0.0)
7	1.1 (1.3)	1.0 (2.1)	0.7 (2.0)	0.3 (0.3)	0.5 (0.7)	0.5 (0.5)	0.1 (0.2)

Note: The values reported in this table are the estimated arithmetic means of the relevant variables across twenty independent replications of the base case scenario. In parentheses below each item in the table is the estimated variance across the replications.

TABLE 4.B.4. Spanish Peaks Base Case Encounters by Trip Length, Thirty Replications

Days on Trip	Number of Parties	Trail Encounters						Camp Encounters	
		Hikers			Riders			Number	Nights
		Small	Medium	Large	Small	Medium	Large		
1	153.7 (61.7)	185.7 (1280.7)	129.9 (806.0)	64.6 (332.9)	27.0 (102.6)	22.9 (70.7)	8.3 (23.1)	0.0 (0.0)	0.0 (0.0)
2	25.5 (18.0)	21.7 (60.2)	15.9 (33.9)	6.1 (9.1)	7.9 (21.8)	5.7 (10.6)	2.1 (2.4)	14.4 (63.3)	9.0 (15.0)
3	23.8 (20.0)	17.6 (31.8)	13.3 (41.9)	5.3 (7.0)	8.4 (21.1)	6.8 (11.5)	3.0 (6.7)	28.5 (176.9)	19.9 (70.2)
4	16.7 (21.7)	11.0 (39.9)	9.2 (18.3)	3.5 (4.7)	5.4 (16.4)	5.1 (9.7)	2.1 (3.5)	32.8 (531.1)	22.1 (126.5)
5	3.5 (2.8)	2.4 (5.1)	1.6 (4.3)	0.8 (1.1)	1.5 (2.1)	1.0 (1.6)	0.4 (0.5)	6.6 (28.0)	5.1 (14.9)
6	1.6 (1.2)	2.6 (7.6)	1.5 (1.6)	1.1 (3.0)	0.2 (0.2)	0.3 (0.3)	0.0 (0.0)	3.2 (10.8)	2.3 (5.2)
7	1.9 (1.6)	2.5 (6.8)	1.7 (2.6)	0.9 (1.1)	0.8 (1.4)	1.0 (2.1)	0.2 (0.3)	6.0 (19.9)	4.2 (21.9)

Note: The values reported in this table are the estimated arithmetic means of the relevant variables across thirty independent replications of the base case scenario. In parentheses below each item in the table is the estimated variance across the replications.

TABLE 4.B.5. Spanish Peaks Base Case Encounters on the Periphery by Party Type, Thirty Replications

Party Type	Number of Parties	Trail Encounters					
		Hikers			Riders		
		Small	Medium	Large	Small	Medium	Large
Hiker							
Small	80.6 (49.8)	95.9 (728.9)	68.2 (155.6)	33.4 (127.2)	15.6 (38.4)	12.5 (37.5)	5.0 (12.7)
Medium	56.6 (34.3)	68.3 (155.6)	45.9 (305.3)	23.0 (63.8)	12.7 (34.8)	9.7 (16.5)	3.5 (4.6)
Large	25.0 (16.7)	33.4 (127.2)	23.0 (63.8)	10.5 (26.3)	5.0 (7.2)	4.7 (3.2)	1.3 (1.7)
Rider							
Small	23.7 (16.4)	15.6 (38.4)	12.8 (33.6)	5.0 (7.2)	5.8 (22.0)	3.9 (5.3)	2.1 (3.6)
Medium	20.4 (9.8)	12.5 (37.5)	9.7 (16.5)	4.7 (3.2)	3.9 (5.3)	4.6 (13.6)	1.9 (2.2)
Large	8.0 (6.2)	5.1 (12.4)	3.5 (4.6)	1.3 (1.7)	2.1 (3.6)	1.8 (2.0)	0.3 (0.5)

Note: The values reported in this table are the estimated arithmetic means of the relevant variables across thirty independent replications of the base case scenario. In parentheses below each item in the table is the estimated variance across the replications.

TABLE 4.B.6. Spanish Peaks Base Case Encounters on the Periphery by Trip Length, Thirty Replications

Days on Trip	Number of Parties	Trail Encounters					
		Hikers			Riders		
		Small	Medium	Large	Small	Medium	Large
1	151.6 (62.4)	182.5 (1303.7)	127.2 (790.2)	63.6 (331.4)	25.4 (109.4)	21.3 (70.7)	7.7 (22.7)
2	23.9 (14.1)	19.9 (58.4)	14.6 (29.6)	5.4 (8.4)	7.2 (22.0)	5.0 (11.1)	1.8 (1.6)
3	20.3 (19.9)	14.0 (25.0)	10.5 (26.1)	4.3 (5.3)	6.7 (14.7)	5.2 (7.6)	2.5 (5.2)
4	11.6 (9.7)	8.1 (25.5)	7.1 (15.1)	2.3 (3.7)	3.9 (13.7)	3.9 (7.7)	1.5 (2.9)
5	3.5 (2.8)	1.9 (3.8)	1.1 (4.2)	0.6 (0.6)	1.3 (1.5)	0.8 (1.0)	0.4 (0.5)
6	1.6 (1.2)	2.4 (7.2)	1.3 (1.6)	1.0 (2.6)	0.2 (0.2)	0.1 (0.2)	0.0 (0.0)
7	1.9 (1.6)	2.1 (4.3)	1.2 (2.2)	0.8 (1.0)	0.6 (1.0)	0.8 (1.7)	0.2 (0.2)

Note: The values reported in this table are the estimated arithmetic means of the relevant variables across thirty independent replications of the base case scenario. In parentheses below each item in the table is the estimated variance across the replications.

CHAPTER 5

SENSITIVITY EXPERIMENTS WITH THE SPANISH PEAKS MODEL

5.1 DESIGN OF THE SENSITIVITY TESTS

This chapter summarizes the results of a set of experiments which examined the effects of altering several of the key parameters in the Spanish Peaks model from their values in the base case. As we noted in chapter 4, the base case or frame of reference is a parameterization of the model that depicts use patterns in the 1970 recreational season. We shall consider variation in three components of the model: (1) the coefficient of variation for the transit time; (2) the total level of use of the area; and (3) the distribution of use across the weeks and days of the simulated season (i.e., the four-week period). Nine experiments have been conducted, each with ten independent replications. Table 5.1 describes these experiments in more detail.

Before proceeding, we should note an important distinction among the three factors considered in our sensitivity tests. The last two factors, namely, the level of use and its distribution, are subject to indirect control through managerial policy. The first factor, by contrast, is a purely technical parameter that may influence the model's ability to replicate behavior. Each control factor was chosen to illustrate how the model might be used in providing additional information for a variety of problems. In the case of the first factor, we are concerned with determining the extent to which the outcomes produced by the model are sensitive to input specifications about which we are uncertain. In a more complete study of a wilderness area, it is reasonable to suggest that before going to the expense of improving certain information used by the model, we determine whether it will affect the estimates in a nontrivial way. The second factor illustrates how one might analyze a managerial policy whose effects are easily quantifiable. That is, control of the use level of an area can be accomplished through a variety of direct and indirect measures. The last factor, the distribution of use, can be considered an example of the results of a management policy whose effect on behavior is not as clear-cut. Here we need to indicate our estimate of the effect of a policy. For example, the model's estimates of the effects of advance registration are dependent on both the estimated impact of the policy on the use pattern and the accuracy of the simulator as a model of behavior.

All factors other than those detailed in the table are constant across the experiments. When the base case experiment is included in this set, we have ten experiments which can be regrouped according to the three factors underlying their respective parameterizations. In this chapter we present the results of tests performed with each encounter measure for each of the four output tables described in chapter 4.[1]

The null hypothesis underlying the tests is that of the one-way analysis-of-variance model.[2] Assume that each encounter measure can be described as follows:

(1) $$E_{ij}^k = u^k + \theta_j^k + \epsilon_{ij}^k$$

where E_{ij}^k = the ith observation of the jth experimental variation for the kth encounter measure

u^k = grand mean of all the parametric variations under study (i.e., number of j's) for the kth encounter measure

θ_j^k = the effect of the variation designated by the jth level on the measured encounters of type k

ϵ_{ij}^k = a random error associated with the kth encounter variable and the ith observation of the jth level of parameterization

In order to understand the model underlying our tests, consider a simple example. One of our tests is to examine the effect of increased levels of usage of the area. In order to do so, we have run the model with five levels of total use, ranging from 180 to 300 parties. The factor distinguishing these experiments is the level of total use. The one-way analysis-of-variance model assumes that there is a difference between the overall or grand mean u^k and the mean for any particular level of use. Thus θ_j^k would be given as:

(2) $$\theta_j^k = u_j^k - u^k$$

Our inferential statements concerning the effects of use on encounters of the kth type are confined to the levels examined. Since the grand mean u^k is the average of means associated with each of the use levels, the net effect of θ_j^k across all levels of use is zero. That is, the sum of the θ_j^k across all j is, by assumption, zero.

---

[1] In what follows we have not presented the tests for the periphery subset of all segments. These tests are available from the authors.

[2] The null hypothesis is that the mean level of each encounter variable does not change with the parameterization of the model.

The error ϵ_{ij}^k reflects the inherent variability in any particular simulation of the model. As we noted in chapter 4, the encounter measures are random variables.[3] Hence any particular experiment must be replicated several times if we are to determine a reasonable estimate of the expected level of each encounter measure. Ten independent replications of each experiment were selected on the basis of our examination of ten, twenty, and thirty replications of each experiment in chapter 4.

There are two types of variation which are measured in this model. For a given level of usage, the variation across the ten replications should reflect only the effects of the random error ϵ_{ij}^k. The variation observed across the levels of usage will reflect both the changes in use levels and the error's contribution. The model assumes that these influences are independent so that there is no contribution made by their joint variation. If use has no effect on the particular encounter measure, then the variation both within use levels and that observed across use levels should measure only the error's effects. Hence, if we were to use each level to estimate the error's variance, it is reasonable to expect them to be approximately equal. The greater the estimate of variance across use levels compared to that within groups, the more likely it is that usage levels have an effect.

Accordingly, it is this basic line of reasoning which underlies the tests presented in this chapter. Clearly this discussion has been heuristic in character, and more detailed treatments are available in a variety of other sources.[4]

Table 5.2 compares the average levels of the encounter variables at each of the five use levels with the data aggregated according to the party-type classification. For some of the encounter variables, an increase in use intensity from 180 parties to 300 parties nearly triples the level of encounters (e.g., small horse party, HP, with small HP, small HP with medium HP). In all categories there is an increase in the average number of encounters each class had with every other class. Two points should be made here. First, these data refer to the set of small hiking parties or whatever category we select and the average number of encounters (across independent replications of the same experiment). They are not the average encounters per individual party. In the next chapter we will examine the data for the "average" party in each class. Second and equally important, the increase in the average number of encounters is not in a smooth monotonic pattern over the five different use levels for several encounter classifications. Given the fairly large variances in the encounter variables, noted in chapter 4, it is reasonable to suspect that the expected levels of some

---

[3] See the discussion in chapter 4, section 4.3, on the effect of the number of replications.

[4] See Henry Scheffé, *The Analysis of Variance* (New York: John Wiley & Sons, 1959).

types of encounters may remain relatively constant over reasonably large changes in the total use pattern. Clearly, part of the reason for this stability is a function of the distributions assigned to incoming parties (i.e., probability distribution for hiking parties and riding parties, and party size) and a part is also due to the character of the probability distributions for different routes.

Table 5.3 presents the average level of encounter for each party type when the coefficient of variation (i.e., ratio of standard deviation to mean) for the transit time is allowed to vary from 5 to 20 percent. The parameterization of these experiments is maintained as that of the base case in all other respects. The results for these changes in the variation in transit time do not appear to exhibit a clear-cut effect on encounters. However, we shall test for differences in the average levels of encounters as the coefficient of variation for transit time changes. These results merely serve to illustrate the relative magnitude of each encounter variable with such a change in the model.

Table 5.4 presents the last set of results. These refer to different use intensities and distributions of use. For the columns labeled A in the table, the distribution of total use over the four weeks and the days within a week corresponds to that of the base case. Those columns labeled B distribute use uniformly across both the weeks of the season and the days within each week. In some cases, there are rather clear differences in the encounter measures for each use level with the two distributions. However, with this information it is not possible to determine whether such discrepancies are simply the results of random factors. This conclusion is, of course, true for each of the three preceding tabular summaries of the sensitivity experiments and provides the motivation for the one-way analysis of variance we have described.

However, it should also be noted that a full sensitivity analysis would require consideration of all possible sources of variation in the level of encounters. Such testing would, therefore, refer to the model as applied to any area. It would require that we consider model parameterizations which were not representative of any existing wilderness area. Because such testing can be expensive and our model can accommodate a large number of possible variations in input data, an evaluation of this scope becomes prohibitive. Moreover, it is not clear that such an evaluation is relevant for those uses of the model which focus on the problems associated with the allocation and management of wildlands and wilderness areas. The sensitivity of the model to only the relevant parameterizations (i.e., those associated with existing areas) is all that need concern us. Our present approach has been to select one such area and work with it, thus further narrowing the range of parameterizations which need to be considered in a study of the sensitivity of the model.

5.2 THE EFFECT OF VARIANCE IN
TRANSIT TIME

As we noted in chapters 3 and 4, the time spent by each party traversing each segment in the area is a function of the particular segment in question, i.e., its physical characteristics, the direction on the segment, the party size and mode of travel, and a random factor. Given the central tendency or expected transit time, based on segment, direction, and party type, the actual transit time is determined by drawing a random variable from a normal distribution with a mean given by the expected transit time and a standard deviation given as some percentage of this mean. At present there is little information as to just what this ratio, designated the co-efficient of variation, ought to be. We have assumed for the base case that it was 12 percent.

In order to determine whether or not more careful attention needs to be given to determining what this ratio is for actual users, we have performed three experiments outlined in table 5.1. They repeat the base case with coefficients of variation in the transit time of 5, 12, and 20 percent. Tables 5.5 and 5.6 present the F statistics from a one-way analysis of variance of these data. Our null hypothesis is that the mean level of each encounter variable does not differ with alterations in the coefficient of variation for transit time. Table 5.5 relates to encounters classified by party type and table 5.6 concerns encounters by trip length. Our results suggest that, for the most part, the differences in encounter levels across the three levels of the coefficient of variation could have been attributed to the stochastic character of the simulation itself. In only two cases, encounters of small riding parties (RP) with small RP and those between small RP and medium RP, do we find a statistically significant difference in the average encounters.

It should be noted that we have held the total use level at 240 parties when the variation in transit time was studied. An examination at higher levels of total use could change these findings. Nonetheless, on the basis of these experiments, at usage levels of the Spanish Peaks during the summer of 1970, the choice of the coefficient of variation in transit time does not appear to exert an appreciable effect on encounters.

5.3 THE EFFECT OF USE INTENSITY ON
ENCOUNTERS

In the first section of this chapter we presented the average number of encounters (across replications) experienced by each group of parties. On the basis of casual empiricism, i.e., comparing these means with increases in use intensity, it appeared that the central tendencies of these encounter measures were, in fact, different according to the level of use intensity. Tables 5.7 and 5.8 present the results of our statistical testing of this null hypothesis (i.e., no differences in the central tendencies of each encounter variable with increases in the total level of use). When the data are summarized by party type, it is clear that both trail and camp encounters are significantly different. This conclusion holds at the 99 percent significance level for most of the encounter variables. Thus, in spite of the fairly substantial variation in the encounter measures across replications of the same experiment, it is possible to detect such differences in the levels of the encounter measures with fairly small changes in the total use level.

Table 5.8 presents the results of these tests applied to the data when they have been aggregated according to trip length. In this case, we find that significant differences in the central tendencies of the encounter measures are apparent as total use increases. However, these differences are not apparent for longer trips (i.e., six- and seven-day trips). Part of the reason for this finding can be attributed to the relatively small number of parties selecting routes which call for trips of this duration. Additionally, it is also likely that they are using the more remote sections of the area. Our route probability distributions suggest that a large fraction of the total use will concentrate on shorter trips and the activity will be maintained in sections of the area which do not interface with these interior areas. Hence, the likelihood of increased encounters with greater total use that follows this pattern is greatly reduced for those parties utilizing the more remote interior sections of Spanish Peaks.

5.4   THE IMPLICATIONS OF USE
PATTERNS FOR ENCOUNTERS

The final set of experiments we shall discuss were conducted to learn whether the level of encounters at each of several use intensities was affected by the distribution of that use across the days of the week and weeks of the four-week simulation period. In order to test these hypotheses, we have applied a one-way analysis of variance to each of three sets of experiments. These sets are distinguished according to the level of total use. Within each set are twenty observations, ten following the use distribution pattern of the base case and ten following a pattern which spreads use uniformly over the days of the week and weeks of the season.

Tables 5.9 and 5.10 present the results of the tests applied for the case of 180 parties using the area. In the first of these tables, encounters by party type are studied, while in the second we have the encounters aggregated according to each party's trip length. In both cases, there do not appear to be important effects on encounters. While some of the encounter measures are significantly different for the two distributions, there is no apparent pattern.

When these same tests are performed at the use intensity corresponding to the base case (i.e., 240 parties), the pattern emerges somewhat more clearly. Tables 5.11 and 5.12 present the results of the one-way analysis of variance for encounters aggregated by party type and by trip length. These findings seem to suggest that use distribution does matter for the parties which are the heaviest users of the area (i.e., small hiking parties). This result is especially clear with the trip-length aggregation format. Here we find that parties with one- or two-day trips have the most to gain when a change in the use of the area is of this character (i.e., short trips of one- or two-day duration).

Tables 5.13 and 5.14 report the results of these tests applied when the total use was 300 parties. In general, the findings with these experiments conform to those of the base case use level. Alteration in the distribution of use, as we have outlined, has its greatest effect on those parties who are in the majority. It happens for our case that they are the small hiking parties. Many of them select one- or two-day trips. However, we would hypothesize that smoothing the pattern of use will generally reduce the encounter records of those taking one-day trips since their use will be concentrated near the entry points where the increased activity resulting from peaked entry patterns will be taking place.

5.5   SUMMARY AND IMPLICATIONS

This chapter has reviewed three sets of experiments designed to gain some insight into the sensitivity of our wilderness simulation results to changes in the model's parameterization. One such set of experiments focused attention on the variability in transit time. Our results suggest that for the base case specification, changes in the coefficient of variation in transit time do not appear to affect measured encounters significantly. These experiments were motivated largely by our lack of information on this parameter and our concern with the effects of the somewhat arbitrary values being specified for it.

Both the remaining analyses are motivated primarily by nontechnical considerations. The analysis of different use intensities has implications for the management of the Spanish Peaks area in the face of increasing demands for wilderness recreation and for the material we outline in chapter 6. Small incremental changes in the total use of the area during our four-week simulated season do show effects on the measured encounters. The variation in encounter experience due solely to random factors does not tend to disguise the effects of increased use. Moreover, the tests suggest that these effects are felt by nearly all groups and in nearly all encounter categories. Only in the classification by trip length do we find the encounters of parties with longer trips relatively insensitive to the total use level. However, this finding does tend to conform to *a priori* expectations, since these groups will have greater opportunity to spend their time in the more remote sections of the area.

Finally, the tests of the effects of use distribution can be viewed as a simple sensitivity analysis for the base case's use distributional assumptions or as an indicator of the effects of certain potential managerial actions such as advance registration or nonprice rationing. One would expect that most of these schemes would focus on smoothing the pattern of arrivals to the area. Tests with three levels of use—180, 240, and 300 parties—suggest that the encounters of those taking short trips (i.e., one or two days) can be reduced by smoothing the distribution of use. This pattern is clearest at the two higher use intensities.

There are many more experiments which might have been conducted with the model.[5] The present set serve to illustrate how further research might be designed and address the issues which we consider most important in the introduction of our traffic simulation model. Clearly, one avenue for further research with the model would be to attempt to estimate a set of response surfaces for the output variables so that we might more completely describe their reactions to simultaneous changes in a variety of the parameters. Chapter 7 outlines some additional avenues for research. The model will provide a rich source of research questions. Our efforts should be viewed as a first step in this research agenda.

---

[5] Detailed summaries of the outputs for each experiment, including the means and variances of each encounter measure, are available on request from the authors.

TABLE 5.1. Outline of the Experiments

Experiment No.	Description
1	Base case scenario[a] with transit time coefficient of variation equal to five percent.
2	Base case scenario with transit time coefficient of variation equal to twenty percent.
3	Base case scenario with a total use of 180 parties.
4	Base case scenario with a total use of 210 parties.
5	Base case scenario with a total use of 270 parties.
6	Base case scenario with a total use of 300 parties.
7	Base case scenario[b] with uniform weekly and daily distributions of use .
8	Base case scenario with uniform weekly and daily distributions of use and a total level of use of 180 parties.
9	Base case scenario with uniform weekly and daily distributions of use and a total level of use of 300 parties.

[a]The Spanish Peaks base case specified the coefficient of variation in transit time to be twelve percent.

[b]The total level of use for the base case was 240 parties during the four-week season which was run.

TABLE 5.2.   Mean Encounter Levels with Alternative Use Intensities[a]

Type of Trail Encounter	Total Number of Parties				
	180	210	240	270	300
Small HP[b] with					
Small H P	52.0	68.8	108.0	144.6	150.2
Medium H P	36.0	53.8	76.1	99.0	103.0
Large H P	21.8	34.7	30.9	44.6	54.1
Small R P	10.4	10.8	15.6	18.2	27.8
Medium R P	5.8	12.2	12.1	19.8	21.4
Large R P	2.5	3.9	5.7	9.8	9.5
Medium HP with					
Medium H P	24.2	43.6	63.5	65.6	57.8
Large H P	15.0	23.7	25.0	28.1	38.0
Small R P	5.8	7.4	10.6	13.6	17.4
Medium R P	4.5	8.0	10.1	13.6	13.1
Large R P	2.4	3.2	3.4	6.7	5.6
Large HP with					
Large H P	11.0	19.4	11.0	11.4	20.4
Small R P	3.1	2.7	7.4	7.4	12.6
Medium R P	1.8	4.5	3.9	5.9	7.6
Large R P	0.9	0.7	1.1	2.7	4.6
Small RP with					
Small R P	5.0	6.0	4.0	7.7	13.0
Medium R P	3.8	3.6	3.4	6.4	9.4
Large R P	1.2	1.9	2.7	3.6	4.1
Medium RP with					
Medium R P	2.4	3.4	4.2	4.2	10.2
Large R P	0.5	2.3	1.5	2.1	2.9
Large RP with					
Large R P	0.4	1.6	1.0	1.0	1.6

[a]This table is based on ten replications of each experiment. A more detailed presentation of these results is found in Appendix A to this chapter.

[b]HP designates Hiking Parties and RP designates Riding Parties.

TABLE 5.3.   Mean Encounter Levels with Alterations in Transit Time Variation

Type of Trail Encounter	Coefficient of Variation		
	5	12	20
Small HP[a] with			
Small H P	84.6	108.0	103.4
Medium H P	61.6	76.1	70.8
Large H P	29.4	30.9	33.9
Small R P	17.1	15.6	17.5
Medium R P	10.9	12.1	33.7
Large R P	4.9	5.7	5.6
Medium HP with			
Medium H P	44.8	63.5	48.0
Large H P	21.2	25.0	21.2
Small R P	13.6	10.6	11.6
Medium R P	13.4	10.1	10.1
Large R P	4.0	3.4	3.4
Large HP with			
Large H P	8.6	11.0	11.0
Small R P	5.7	7.4	5.4
Medium R P	4.2	3.9	4.0
Large R P	1.5	1.1	1.2
Small RP with			
Small R P	8.8	4.0	9.8
Medium R P	8.6	3.4	7.3
Large R P	3.0	2.7	2.8
Medium RP with			
Medium R P	5.2	4.2	6.4
Large R P	1.9	1.5	1.2
Large RP with			
Large R P	0.2	1.0	0.4

[a]HP designates Hiking Parties and RP designates Riding Parties.

TABLE 5.4. Mean Encounter Levels with Different Use Levels and Distributions

| Type of Trail Encounter | USE LEVEL | | | | | |
| | 180 | | 240 | | 300 | |
	A	B	A	B	A	B
Small HP[a] with						
Small H P	52.0	48.2	108.0	65.4	150.2	105.0
Medium H P	36.0	27.3	76.1	44.8	103.0	76.1
Large H P	21.8	18.2	30.9	24.2	54.1	36.0
Small R P	10.4	5.8	15.6	11.8	27.8	19.5
Medium R P	5.8	4.1	12.1	9.9	21.4	19.4
Large R P	2.5	2.5	5.7	3.9	9.5	7.0
Medium HP with						
Medium H P	24.2	16.4	63.5	32.2	57.8	50.6
Large H P	15.0	10.4	25.0	15.4	38.0	27.9
Small R P	5.8	5.0	10.6	9.6	17.4	15.6
Medium R P	4.5	4.5	10.1	7.0	13.1	13.0
Large R P	2.4	2.1	3.4	2.1	5.6	6.6
Large HP with						
Large H P	11.0	4.2	11.0	7.6	20.4	14.6
Small R P	3.1	2.5	7.4	4.3	12.6	7.6
Medium R P	1.8	2.6	3.9	3.3	7.6	7.2
Large R P	0.9	0.9	1.1	1.3	4.6	2.4
Small RP[a] with						
Small R P	5.0	2.0	4.0	4.0	13.0	8.2
Medium R P	3.8	1.9	3.4	6.5	9.4	6.7
Large R P	1.2	1.8	2.7	2.3	4.1	3.6
Medium RP with						
Medium R P	2.4	1.8	4.2	3.2	10.2	5.2
Large R P	0.5	1.0	1.5	1.5	2.9	3.2
Large RP with						
Large R P	0.4	0.4	1.0	0.4	1.6	0.8

[a]HP designates Hiking Party and RP designates Riding Party.

TABLE 5.5. Test of the Effects of Coefficient of Variation in Transit Time — Encounters by Party Type

Party Type	Number of Parties	Trail Encounters						Camp Encounters
		Hikers			Riders			
		Small	Medium	Large	Small	Medium	Large	
Hikers								
Small	0.51	2.19	2.76	0.69	0.26	1.13	0.25	1.14
Medium	0.61	2.76	2.07	0.95	0.50	1.71	0.17	0.50
Large	2.49	0.69	0.95	0.51	0.72	0.04	0.29	0.81
Riders								
Small	0.44	0.26	0.50	0.72	6.28[a]	4.51[b]	0.04	0.03
Medium	0.57	1.13	1.71	0.04	4.51[b]	0.99	0.47	0.74
Large	0.55	0.25	0.17	0.29	0.04	0.47	1.67	0.54

Note: This table presents the calculated F statistics for a one-way analysis of variance. $F_{(2,27)_{\alpha=.05}} = 3.35$, $F_{(2,27)_{\alpha=.01}} = 5.49$.

a   Significant at the .01 level.
b   Significant at the .05 level.

TABLE 5.6. Test of the Effects of Coefficient of Variation in Transit Time—Encounters by Trip Length

Days on Trip	Number of Parties	Trail Encounters Hikers			Trail Encounters Riders			Camp Encounters	
		Small	Medium	Large	Small	Medium	Large	Number	Nights
1	1.04	1.86	2.53	1.43	1.09	1.52	0.37	--	--
2	1.38	0.12	0.13	0.08	0.58	2.37	0.47	0.19	0.15
3	0.26	1.57	0.85	0.04	0.55	2.06	0.34	1.16	1.24
4	0.30	3.27	1.73	0.85	2.42	1.87	0.08	0.60	0.10
5	0.96	1.79	0.52	0.00	1.93	0.00	0.43	0.38	0.36
6	0.18	2.24	0.31	0.71	0.00	0.22	2.10	0.36	0.07
7	3.83	0.63	0.63	0.12	0.53	0.14	1.73	0.89	1.11

Note: This table presents the calculated F statistics for a one-way analysis of variance. $F_{(2,27)_{\alpha=.05}} = 3.35$, $F_{(2,27)_{\alpha=.01}} = 5.49$.

TABLE 5.7. Test of the Effects of Use Intensity — Encounters by Party Type

Type of Party	Number of Parties	Trail Encounters Hikers Small	Hikers Medium	Hikers Large	Riders Small	Riders Medium	Riders Large	Camp Encounters
Hikers								
Small	69.84[a]	21.99[a]	42.47[a]	12.84[a]	11.51[a]	13.10[a]	7.77[a]	3.98[a]
Medium	38.93[a]	42.47[a]	14.68[a]	7.59[a]	7.66[a]	5.62[a]	4.42[a]	3.18[b]
Large	11.24[a]	12.84[a]	7.59[a]	5.17[a]	5.72[a]	5.19[a]	6.61[a]	0.62
Riders								
Small	10.37[a]	11.51[a]	7.66[a]	5.72[a]	5.41[a]	7.05[a]	3.43[b]	3.06[b]
Medium	11.72[a]	13.10[a]	5.62[a]	5.72[a]	7.05[a]	3.72[b]	2.85[b]	4.99[a]
Large	3.97[a]	7.77[a]	4.42[a]	6.61[a]	3.43[b]	2.85[b]	0.75	1.72

Note: This table presents the calculated F statistics for a one-way analysis of variance. $F_{(4,45)_{\alpha=.05}} = 2.61$, $F_{(4,45)_{\alpha=.01}} = 3.83$.

a Significant at the .01 level.

b Significant at the .05 level.

TABLE 5.8.　Test of the Effects of Use Intensity — Encounters by Trip Length

Days on Trip	Number of Parties	Trail Encounters						Camp Encounters	
		Hikers			Riders			Number	Nights
		Small	Medium	Large	Small	Medium	Large		
1	164.82^a	27.49^a	30.11^a	18.97^a	9.43^a	10.82^a	6.96^a	--	--
2	16.10^a	17.55^a	12.20^a	1.63	9.34^a	4.84^a	3.31^b	5.18^a	10.21^a
3	8.39^a	7.14^a	7.75^a	5.53^a	7.96^a	4.76^a	3.31^b	4.02^a	6.21^a
4	4.60^a	7.41^a	4.60^a	5.09^a	3.88^a	3.57^b	1.57	3.67^b	4.54^a
5	4.10^a	5.38^a	3.28^b	1.14	0.59	0.95	2.31	1.58	1.80
6	0.52	1.05	1.70	0.47	1.25	2.37	1.00	1.29	1.62
7	4.44^a	1.32	0.78	0.38	1.46	1.28	1.34	0.58	1.05

Note: This table presents the calculated F statistics for a one-way analysis of variance.　$F_{(4, 45)_{\alpha=.05}} = 2.61$, $F_{(4, 45)_{\alpha=.01}} = 3.83$.

a　Significant at the .01 level.

b　Significant at the .05 level.

TABLE 5.9. Test of the Effects of Use Distribution, Total Use of 180 Parties — Encounters by Party Type

Type of Party	Number of Parties	Trail Encounters						Camp Encounters
		Hikers			Riders			
		Small	Medium	Large	Small	Medium	Large	
Hikers								
Small	7.71[a]	0.27	5.27[a]	0.95	11.47[b]	1.38	--	1.76
Medium	0.13	5.27[a]	3.01	3.76	0.52	--	0.09	5.86[a]
Large	0.99	0.95	3.76	6.87	0.28	1.80	--	1.90
Riders								
Small	2.86	11.47[b]	0.52	0.28	4.55[a]	3.76	1.19	0.03
Medium	1.95	1.38	--	1.80	3.76	0.28	1.55	1.97
Large	--	--	0.09	--	1.19	1.55	--	0.01

Note: This table presents the calculated F statistics for a one-way analysis of variance $F_{(1, 18)}{}_{\alpha=.05} = 4.41$, $F_{(1, 18)}{}_{\alpha=.01} = 8.29$.

a Significant at the .05 level.

b Significant at the .01 level.

TABLE 5.10. Test of the Effects of Use Distribution, Total Use of 180 Parties — Encounters by Trip Length

Days on Trip	Number of Parties	Trail Encounters						Camp Encounters	
		Hikers			Riders			Number	Nights
		Small	Medium	Large	Small	Medium	Large		
1	0.61	3.86	4.66[a]	2.85	13.66[b]	0.09	0.13	---	---
2	0.07	0.57	1.94	3.15	3.23	1.57	0.18	7.21[a]	6.49[a]
3	1.81	0.01	---	0.17	0.32	0.25	0.05	2.79	0.94
4	0.10	0.69	3.52	0.23	0.83	0.97	8.82[b]	0.15	0.98
5	0.65	0.13	0.14	0.34	1.17	---	0.57	1.94	1.55
6	1.44	2.00	3.12	1.38	1.53	---	---	2.76	3.00
7	0.94	0.15	3.23	0.24	6.00[a]	0.42	1.00	0.01	0.11

Note: This table presents the calculated F statistics for a one-way analysis of variance $F(1, 18)_{\alpha=.05} = 4.41$, $F(1, 18)_{\alpha=.01} = 8.29$.

a   Significant at the .05 level.

b   Significant at the .01 level.

TABLE 5.11.   Test of the Effects of Use Distribution, Total Use of 240 Parties — Encounters by Party Type

Type of Party	Number of Parties	Trail Encounters						Camp Encounters
		Hikers			Riders			
		Small	Medium	Large	Small	Medium	Large	
Hikers								
Small	1.07	39.33[a]	41.90[a]	3.14	3.30	1.03	3.35	3.64
Medium	0.59	41.90[a]	18.52[a]	7.17[b]	0.20	3.22	1.70	0.93
Large	0.49	3.14	7.17[b]	2.36	3.22	0.28	0.10	12.04[a]
Riders								
Small	4.34	3.30	0.20	3.22	--	2.54	0.21	0.22
Medium	1.19	1.03	3.22	0.28	2.54	0.41	--	--
Large	1.29	3.35	1.70	0.10	0.21	--	1.33	0.09

Note: This table presents the calculated F statistics for a one-way analysis of variance $F(1, 18)_{\alpha=.05} = 4.41$, $F(1, 18)_{\alpha=.01} = 8.29$.

a   Significant at the .01 level.

b   Significant at the .05 level.

TABLE 5.12. Test of the Effects of Use Distribution, Total Use of 240 Parties — Encounters by Trip Length

Days on Trip	Number of Parties	Trail Encounters Hikers Small	Hikers Medium	Hikers Large	Riders Small	Riders Medium	Riders Large	Camp Encounters Number	Nights
1	0.80	63.34[a]	27.98[a]	6.73[b]	1.22	1.90	0.20	--	--
2	0.49	7.33[b]	12.75[a]	1.76	--	0.37	5.04[b]	0.65	0.25
3	1.94	2.14	7.36[b]	0.40	1.23	2.45	0.02	11.82[a]	9.80[a]
4	1.73	0.09	2.15	0.92	--	1.71	3.62	1.75	0.01
5	4.77[b]	12.21[a]	0.33	0.90	0.45	0.53	0.65	--	0.09
6	0.03	1.07	0.14	0.06	--	1.00	1.00	0.04	0.03
7	2.98	1.78	2.43	0.21	0.05	3.94	1.44	0.93	1.46

Note: This table presents the calculated F statistics for a one-way analysis of variance $F_{(1, 18)_{\alpha=.05}} = 4.41$, $F_{(1, 18)_{\alpha=.01}} = 8.29$.

a   Significant at the .01 level.

b   Significant at the .05 level.

TABLE 5.13. Test of the Effects of Use Distribution, Total Use of 300 Parties — Encounters by Party Type

Type of Party	Number of Parties	Trail Encounters						Camp Encounters
		Hikers			Riders			
		Small	Medium	Large	Small	Medium	Large	
Hikers								
Small	0.02	8.40[a]	13.17[a]	19.99[a]	8.76[a]	0.75	1.25	0.26
Medium	0.48	13.17[a]	0.93[a]	6.64[b]	0.57	--	0.53	0.01
Large	0.28	19.99[a]	6.64[b]	2.94	3.13	0.04	3.01	0.27
Riders								
Small	--	8.76[a]	0.57	3.13	4.34	2.34	0.26	6.23[b]
Medium	0.21	0.75	--	0.04	2.34	2.29	0.09	4.94[b]
Large	0.11	1.25	0.53	3.01	0.26	0.01	1.03	0.92

Note: This table presents the calculated F statistics for a one-way analysis of variance. $F_{(1, 18)_{\alpha=.05}} = 4.41$, $F_{(1, 18)_{\alpha=.01}} = 8.29$.

a Significant at the .01 level.

b Significant at the .05 level.

TABLE 5.14. Test of the Effects of Use Distribution, Total Use of 300 Parties — Encounters by Trip Length

Days on Trip	Number of Parties	Trail Encounters						Camp Encounters	
		Hikers			Riders			Number	Nights
		Small	Medium	Large	Small	Medium	Large		
1	0.05	9.08[a]	11.06[a]	27.85[a]	7.30[b]	0.91	0.18	—	—
2	0.73	6.33[b]	0.78	1.27	2.09	4.25	0.69	0.60	0.28
3	4.40	0.32	0.27	0.34	0.42	0.05	0.45	0.04	—
4	0.02	2.22	0.50	0.04	2.31	1.68	0.34	4.41[b]	1.44
5	7.51	0.10	4.56[b]	1.72	0.99	0.07	0.08	0.44	1.04
6	0.33	0.34	0.32	0.80	0.11	0.36	1.00	0.05	0.05
7	0.31	0.41	1.11	0.95	0.10	0.28	0.20	0.05	0.05

Note: This table presents the calculated F statistics for a one-way analysis of variance $F_{(1,\ 18)_{\alpha=.05}} = 4.41$, $F_{(1,\ 18)_{\alpha=.01}} = 8.29$.

[a]   Significant at the .01 level.

[b]   Significant at the .05 level.

CHAPTER 6

USE OF THE WILDERNESS SIMULATOR WITH WILLINGNESS-TO-PAY RELATIONSHIPS

6.1 INTRODUCTION

In chapter 1 we outlined a conceptual framework for addressing problems associated with allocation and management of wildlands and wilderness resources; we provided the background to motivate the development of a simulator. Our emphasis has been to illustrate its application to an existing wilderness area and to examine some of the properties of the simulation model developed to mimic the travel behavior of wilderness users. We have also provided a general structure for analyzing the optimal recreation capacity of a given wilderness area. While it is beyond the scope of the present study to attempt to determine the optimal capacity of the Spanish Peaks Wilderness Area, we shall illustrate in this chapter how the simulator can be used, in conjunction with information on the preferences of wilderness users for reduction of encounters with other parties, to determine the optimal capacity—and also to examine the costs and benefits of various management practices employed for this purpose.

Before proceeding with the analysis, it might be useful to consider the principal approaches to modeling the character of individual demands for outdoor recreation and the suitability of these approaches for the problem we address, i.e., accounting for the effects of congestion on the demand for wilderness recreation. Cicchetti, Fisher, and Smith (1973) distinguish three approaches to modeling the demand for recreation. While the methods are not mutually inconsistent, typically the availability of data limits the choice to a single approach. Hence, the methods have been identified according to the source of data usually associated with the approach. They have been designated as site-specific, population-specific, and site-specific-user models.

The first of these approaches is often referred to as a travel-cost model. In general this model uses information indexed by origin zone for the visitors to a given recreational facility. Thus the model begins with the basic assumption that to acquire the services of the recreational site, users must transport themselves to it. If the quality of the services provided by the area can be assumed constant over the time period when the visits are recorded, and each user stays the same amount of time on site, then it is suggested that individuals reveal their willingness to pay for the site's services by transporting themselves to the site, and the travel costs can *ceteris paribus* serve as reasonably good surrogates for the prices each individual pays for the services of the site. Since most areas have only nominal user charges, and the time cost may also be assumed to be roughly proportional to the distance traveled, the assumptions have appeared reasonable to most researchers. Moreover, the basic structure has seemed to be quite robust in a variety of applications.[1]

Unfortunately, the assumption of constant quality is untenable for our purpose. That is, our objective is to determine *the effects of quality* on a representative individual's valuation of the experience. While there appear to be a variety of ways in which this approach might have been used to indirectly infer the disbenefits associated with congestion, they were not utilized because of limitations of data or theory associated with each. Rather than enumerating an exhaustive list of these alternatives, we shall cite several examples and the assumptions necessary to fit each to our purpose. One approach would call for estimating travel-cost–demand relations for each of several wilderness areas with different use intensities for the season or period under study. The differences in the price response might then be considered an indirect measure of the congestion effect. This inference requires that we assume the areas and their respective demanders are identical except for the levels of use. It seems clear that this assumption is completely unrealistic and that following this scheme would likely misrepresent the effects of congestion.

An alternative scheme would call for analyzing the demands for a given area during peak and off-peak use periods. While the information necessary for such an analysis is not available, there are additional considerations. Primary among them is our inability to define the complete function for response to congestion. That is, with only two levels of use we must infer the full nature of an individual's reactions to congestion. Again, the assumptions necessarily involved are too stringent to make the results useful.

The second approach to measuring the character of the demand for recreation has been designated the population-specific model. Since this approach focuses on the determinants of individual recreation participation patterns without detailed information on the quality and character of the facilities used, it is not suited to our objective. While it is reasonable to

---

[1] See Knetsch (1974) and Smith (1975b) for more complete discussions of the limitations associated with the model. Smith (1975a) has also examined the model when applied to estimating the demand for wilderness recreation at the Desolation Area and has found some problems with the interpretation of the estimates.

assume that an individual's decisions on his recreational activities will be affected by his anticipation of congestion at the site (or sites) he will use, past surveys have not provided sufficient information for one to infer the nature of the congestion's effect. It should be noted that this does not mean surveys could not be designed to solicit such information. However, the character of such procedures would necessarily resemble the approach to modeling recreational behavior that was selected by Cicchetti and Smith (1973) to measure the adverse effects of congestion on wilderness users. This approach has been designated in the previous taxonomy as site-specific user studies.

These studies have generally sought information from the users of a given recreational area on their attitudes and satisfaction with the services provided by the area. Those individuals who were not at the site during the time of the survey, either because they do not use the site or do not participate in the activities it permits, are not considered in the evaluation. This approach, when used to examine the users' reactions to hypothetical experiences at an area they are familiar with, appears reasonably well suited to the problem.

Cicchetti and Smith (1973) developed it further, extending the work of others in this area so as to allow a wide range of hypothetical conditions to be applied to a limited sample. Since their analysis focused on users of the Spanish Peaks Area and was designed to use measures of congestion consistent with the simulator's outputs, we shall illustrate in what follows how the two research efforts might be used together.

The measure of satisfaction used in this interrogation was willingness to pay. At least two reasons might be suggested to question the validity of responses to such hypothetical questions. First, as Samuelson (1954) has pointed out, an individual has an incentive to understate his willingness to pay for a publicly good provided because he may believe that he can continue to enjoy it without being assessed his full consumer surplus. Second, the individual may strategize from an alternative perspective, overstating his willingness to pay, if he is sure he will not have to pay, in the hope that such misinformation will increase the supply.

The only evidence on these issues was provided by Bohm (1972) in an experimental study of consumer responses to alternative questions soliciting their willingness to pay. His findings suggest that there was not a significant difference in the maximum revealed willingness to pay across the types of questions. Since they included forms designed to elicit the opposing biases, his findings seem to suggest that the distortions are not likely to be significant.

The willingness-to-pay measure has been adopted over some non-monetary measures because the former are more easily aggregated both across individuals and across days of a given trip. Thus an aggregate benefit function comparable to that derived in chapter 1 can be constructed from individual willingness-to-pay functions. Of course, these advantages do not imply that aggregate willingness to pay is completely free of interpersonal considerations, since it is dependent on the distribution of income. There are a couple of possible responses to such objections. First, it is possible to assume an exogenous, socially sanctioned distribution of income and base the aggregate willingness-to-pay function on it. Or we might note the positive relation between participation in wilderness recreation and income (and education). Such recreation can be classed as a "luxury" good, one for which the demand rises more than proportionately with income (see Brown, 1971 and some limited evidence in Smith, 1975a).

Thus there are some distinct advantages from the site-specific user model if we are attempting to illustrate how the logic outlined in chapter 1 for economic management of low-density recreational areas might be used effectively. In section 6.2 we briefly summarize the Cicchetti–Smith results and their interpretation. Section 6.3 discusses how the estimated willingness-to-pay relations and the simulation outputs might be used together. The last section summarizes the results.

6.2   THE ESTIMATION OF CONGESTION EFFECTS ON INDIVIDUAL WILLINGNESS TO PAY

The specification of individual willingness-to-pay functions for wilderness recreation follows directly from the theory of consumer behavior. Cicchetti and Smith (1976) note that there are several approaches to including the effects of congestion within these models. From the standpoint of the derived willingness-to-pay functions, these alternatives are observationally equivalent. That is, the information available to specify the willingness-to-pay function is no more restrictive with one format than with another. Rather than discuss each alternative in detail, we shall briefly indicate two representative approaches to the problem. The first of these follows from Oakland's (1972) work and calls for including congestion as an argument of the individual's utility function. If congestion is outside the individual's control but subject to change, it will affect his demands for goods and services, particularly those where he can directly experience its effects (i.e., wilderness recreation). That is, the demand function is usually defined as the quantities an individual will demand at given prices. A willingness-to-pay function simply alters causality in that it is the amount an individual would be willing to pay for each level of consumption. Congestion affects the quality of the services being consumed and hence should affect the individual's willingness to pay for them.

A second example can be given which differs from the first only in the "mechanics" of specifying how congestion enters the consumer choice framework. It begins with the Becker (1965) household production model and specifies congestion as an input that influences the individual's ability to produce recreational service flows. In this model, the individual combines the services of a recreational site, market goods and services, and his time. In determining the effects of congestion and willingness-to-pay relations, it is necessary to focus on what effects congestion has on the derived demand for the site's services. *A priori* we expect that higher levels of congestion will reduce the marginal product of the site's services in the production of recreational service flows and therefore the derived demand function. The willingness-to-pay function can be treated as a representation of one of the derived demand equations. Since we do not have sufficient information from theory to distinguish between these models and other competing alternatives, it seems reasonable to begin the analysis with the statement of a willingness-to-pay relation; this is the basic approach Cicchetti and Smith take.

While there are no exact theoretical guidelines to follow in specifying the willingness-to-pay function, Cicchetti and Smith's examination of alternative forms favored a semilog function, with the log of willingness to pay a function of the characteristics of the experience and the individual.

Before discussing the results in detail, it is important to consider the process of data collection. As we noted at the outset, direct solicitation of willingness to pay for hypothetical experiences has a number of problems. These problems may be more acute for wilderness users, since they are in many cases unfamiliar with the notion of a price for wilderness recreational services, viewing them as a right.[2] Additionally, in many cases such experiences form an important part of the individual's life and he cannot isolate a valuation for them. In effect, they seem essential. The evidence we cited from Bohm provides some support for the fact that the conventionally considered response biases may not be very large. A second, more specific, source of bias is one for which we do not have an answer. Cicchetti and Smith examined the characteristics of those respondents who could and did quantify their willingness to pay for wilderness recreation in contrast to those who did not and found that a general characterization of the socioeconomic attributes of those who quantified their willingness to pay was not possible.[3]

Aside from the problems associated with the revelation of preferences by the individual, there remains an equally if not more important problem to be resolved in the survey research itself. The data base for the study consisted of a sample of users of the Spanish Peaks Area during the sum-

---

[2] The respondents to the Cicchetti–Smith survey in several cases included comments along with their questionnaires suggesting that they viewed the use of wilderness as their "right" and could not envision a setting in which it would not be available.

[3] Cicchetti and Smith (1976), chapter 3.

mer of 1970. The sample had been compiled to examine a number of other issues by Robert Lucas and George Stankey. The names of the respondents were available to Cicchetti and Smith for recontact on further issues in a mailed questionnaire.

Since it was unreasonable to expect that the actual experiences of these sampled individuals would exhibit the diversity (in terms of the numbers and types of encounters) necessary for estimation of willingness-to-pay relationships, a set of hypothetical wilderness trip encounter experiences was defined. Conventional survey research would suggest that all of these experiences might be asked of each sampled individual. Such a strategy implied that each individual would be asked to evaluate his willingness to pay in 120 to 200 hypothetical experiences. Pretest experience with the questionnaire by Lucas and Stankey suggested that responses to even thirty questions of this type exceeded the response capability of tested subjects. Consequently, some alternative means had to be found that would obtain responses to the full range of experiences and yet limit the number of questions addressed to each individual. Cicchetti and Smith developed a procedure for sampling from the set of all questions and asking each individual a small sample of independent questions about hypothetical trip experiences. Their justification for this procedure is drawn from the literature on experimental design in statistics. In this discipline the problems associated with selecting a set of values for the independent variables of some response surface are addressed. The choice of any design or sampling procedure (i.e., which type of wilderness experiences should be surveyed) can be viewed as a tradeoff between the bias and variance associated with estimates of the response surface parameters. Given the inability to specify the exact form of the willingness-to-pay function, Cicchetti and Smith suggest that full coverage of all types of hypothetical trip experiences appeared to represent the best design.

This full coverage of hypothetical wilderness experiences, sometimes called design points, was accomplished by assigning them to each individual with equal probability. Reactions to five such experiences were asked of each individual sampled. Each resulted from an independent drawing from the set of all possible trip encounter experiences within the selected range. There was, however, a check to be sure that reaction to the same experience was not asked more than once of the same individual.[4]

Approximately 600 questionnaires were sent to a sample of those who used the Spanish Peaks Area during the summer of 1970. After two mail-

---

[4] Thus strictly speaking, the event selection of question two is not independent of the selection of question one. However, the conditional probability that question two will call for response to any given hypothetical scenario with the check for duplication is approximately equal to the probability of that scenario being selected for question one (e.g., in our case the probability of any one hypothetical experience for the first question is $1/60$ and for any other scenario, of those remaining, for the second is $1/59$).

ings, over 40 percent of the mailed questionnaires were returned. Several functional forms for the willingness-to-pay functions were examined. On the basis of *a priori* theory the semilog specification for individual willingness to pay has considerable appeal. Under a linear specification, each of the encounter measures taken into account has a constant marginal effect. This implies, for example, that the estimated effect of the last trail encounter is constant regardless of the level of such encounters experienced. In contrast, the semilog specification allows for a diminishing marginal effect of the last encounter as the total number experienced increases.

The Cicchetti–Smith study examines the effect of trail encounters and the number of nights of at least one camp encounter on individual willingness to pay. It considers the effects of whether or not the encounters are with hiking parties or with riding parties, but does not consider mixtures of trail encounters with hiking parties and riding parties. Moreover, the study does not attempt to differentiate between encounters occurring close to the trail head and those occurring in the interior sections of the area. Thus the congestion measures examined in the willingness-to-pay analysis are not as detailed as those available in the simulation outputs, and we must consider the aggregation of encounter measures. This problem may be important to the extent the distinctions in the simulation model's outputs reflect differences in the disruptive effects of the encounters. *A priori* we cannot develop a weighting scheme, since a more comprehensive analysis of individual preferences would be necessary to determine whether the different encounters have different effects on willingness to pay. For this study, a variety of simplifying assumptions will be made; these are discussed in greater detail in the next section.

Table 6.1 gives the "best" equation in the semilog specification from the analysis of encounters with hiking parties and table 6.2 provides the "best" equation when the encounters are postulated to occur with riding parties. Both the ordinary least squares and the Aitken generalized least squares estimates are presented.[5] In general, the empirical findings are encouraging. Both trail and camp encounters matter, though the authors note there is no statistically significant difference in their measured effects on willingness to pay. Given the reservations we noted concerning the potential bias in solicited willingness to pay, as well as the low overall explanatory power of the estimated willingness-to-pay functions, it is reasonable to be skeptical of the predictions from these estimated relationships. In other words, we are not confident that these equations will provide good estimates of the level of individual willingness to pay.[6] They should,

---

[5] See Cicchetti and Smith (1976), chapter 4, for a discussion of the construction of the GLS estimator.

[6] There is also a problem associated with the form of the dependent variable. Our estimates of the log of willingness to pay will be unbiased, but the antilog transformation causes the estimated willingness to pay to understate its expected value. This

however, indicate the change in willingness to pay with a change in our quality measures. Consequently, if we assume the actual willingness to pay is a scalar function of the estimated functions, it is possible to use the latter to determine the optimal use intensity. The estimate of aggregate benefits, however, should not be considered an accurate measure of the level of benefits derived from the use of the area.

6.3   THE USE OF THE TRAFFIC SIMULATION MODEL AND WILLINGNESS-TO-PAY FUNCTIONS

The first of the simplifications which should be considered stems from the problem of aggregating the estimated individual willingness-to-pay functions. We are concerned with only the length of stay and encounter variables, so that we would like to aggregate over all individuals classified according to income, sex, and weeks of paid vacation. Assuming we knew the multivariate frequency distribution for users when classified according to these factors, we would simply add up (or integrate in the case of a multivariate density function) the relevant cells to construct our aggregate willingness-to-pay relationship. Probably the most important of these factors is the postulated distribution of users over all income classes. As we suggested in the discussion at the outset of this chapter, it is likely that the results will be sensitive to the assumptions we make with respect to the income distribution. Since our efforts are meant to be illustrative rather than definitive, we have selected the simplest aggregation scheme. We assume that all individuals have the same income, sex, and weeks of paid vacation as the mean values of our sample. It should, however, be noted that the methods we have utilized can be used with equal facility for any preassigned distribution for these factors.

With these assumptions our aggregate willingness-to-pay function (AWP) is given in equation (1).

(1) $AWP = N\exp(0.357 + 0.780\,x_1 - 0.069\,x_1^2 - 0.083\,x_2 - 0.152\,x_3)$

where N = the total number of users
  x_1 = length of the trip in days
  x_2 = number of trail encounters per day
  x_3 = number of nights of camp encounters

As the coefficients of (1) indicate, we have selected the generalized least squares estimates of the willingness-to-pay function.

---

follows from the fact that the expected value of any strictly convex transformation of a random variable is less than the transformation of the expected value. Since the exponential function is convex, the predictions for willingness to pay will be biased downward.

Before discussing the relationship between variables x_1, x_2, and x_3 and the outputs of the simulator, it is necessary to consider the character of the data we are utilizing to estimate an aggregate willingness-to-pay–use intensity relationship. The coefficients of the willingness-to-pay function (reported in tables 6.1 and 6.2) are random variables. Since the aggregate willingness to pay is a function of these estimates, it also is a random variable. Similarly, as we noted in chapter 4, the encounter estimates are also random variables. We have utilized the sample mean (over ten replications) of each encounter variable as a measure of the expected value for that variable. When we attempt to link these two estimates, the result will be a random variable whose probability distribution is unknown. Moreover, we cannot characterize its variance. The value is a nonlinear function of random variables, thereby making a definition of its variance difficult. In what follows we shall treat our estimates *as if* they were parameters and consequently we will not address these issues. Such a policy should not imply that they are not important, but rather that they are outside the scope of this inquiry. We have sought to illustrate a methodology for using the model and have deliberately simplified the framework.

We noted in chapters 2 and 4 that the simulator provides a variety of summary statistics. The set of tables that will be of particular interest to us in developing the use of aggregate willingness to pay with the simulator results is the summary of parties' encounter records by trip length. These tables indicate the number of parties selecting trips of a particular length and the kinds of encounter experiences the group in each class had as a whole.

In chapter 5 we analyzed the effects of use intensity on group experiences. Now our attention must focus on the expected experience for each member of the group. In this case, each group refers to the set of parties having a particular trip length. The reported encounters refer to the records of all parties and not any single one of them. Consequently, we need to estimate what each individual party can expect in order to derive what kind of experience each individual user can expect.

The process of estimating what the character of the experience might be is reasonably straightforward. Each parameterization (in this case use intensity with all other characteristics conforming to that of the base case) of the model was repeated ten times for ten independent drawings from the underlying population. The average across these replications was then computed for each encounter measure in the trip length tables. These estimates were then compiled for encounters with all hiking parties and all riding parties. Since our willingness-to-pay function does not distinguish the effects of differences in the size of the encountered party and we had no *a priori* estimates of the relative effects, we simply aggregated the encounters with small, medium, and large hiking parties and did the same for riding parties for all parties of each trip length. These aggregates were then divided by the average number of parties selecting routes of each length from one to seven days, thus providing an estimate of the number of trail encounters and nights of camp encounters to be expected by each party for a given total use intensity. Table 6.3 provides these estimates for each use intensity.

Trail encounters are entered as the average per day rather than for the trip as a whole in the willingness-to-pay functions. Thus the estimates of the expected trail encounters have been adjusted to conform to a per day measure for parties with each trip length. Since the estimated willingness-to-pay functions did not distinguish between trail encounters with hiking parties and riding parties, the two estimates must be aggregated. We have assumed in our aggregation that differential weight is given to encounters with riding parties. These weights were determined by taking the ratio of the measured effect of trail encounters with riding parties from table 6.2 relative to that for hiking parties. Clearly, this procedure is *ad hoc*. In the absence of better information on the relative impact of these two kinds of encounters, the choice was either to assume they have equal effect or to attempt to account for a difference. Stankey's (1972) research suggests that such a difference does exist, so that a rough accounting of it appears to be desirable.

Casual inspection of table 6.3 reveals that we are not necessarily assured of smooth increases in the encounter measures. For example, comparison of the number of nights with at least one camp encounter per party across use intensities indicates that in many cases there is a decline from initial levels with increases in use intensity. There are a number of ways one might explain this finding. First, and perhaps most important, the stochastic effects on the model's observed outcomes are not inconsequential. Despite averaging across replications, there may well be enough "noise" in our measures that we fail to perceive the smooth pattern which may describe "average" encounters per party and total use levels.

Second, increases in the use intensity do not assure proportionate increases in the number of parties taking various trips and hence staying on site for the different periods. The selection is probabilistic, and for particular routes increases in use may be readily tolerated without generating congestion in interior segments of the area. We might assume that the principal effects are at the peripheries so that trail encounters reflect this effect more readily.

Finally, this table does not indicate the number of parties which might have been expected to have the average nights of camp encounters. If the number is small, then we might expect that the sequence of random factors attached to trail segment times and camp departure times might be quite important to the model's observed outcomes.

It seems reasonable to argue that there are likely to be other explanations of the absence of a smooth pattern. The primary point is that the stochastic effects associated with most actions in the model prevent rationalizing the model's outputs.

With these data it was possible to calculate the amount an average individual with a given trip length would be willing to pay for the expected experience at each use intensity level. In order to obtain a measure of aggregate benefits for reviewing the respective use intensities, it was necessary to aggregate over trip lengths. In this case we distributed the total use level (e.g., 180 parties, 210 parties, and so on) over the respective trip length categories according to the average relative frequencies calculated over the ten replications of each experiment. Finally, it was necessary to assign an estimate to the average number of individuals in each party of each trip length. We have assumed three individuals in all cases. Table 6.4 reports the results under these assumptions. Should the latter assumption be changed to two, the corresponding aggregate benefits are simply a multiple ($\frac{2}{3}$) of that reported in the table.

Two estimates of aggregate willingness to pay have been calculated for each of the five use intensity levels examined in our earlier experiments. The first of these included all encounters in the process of adjusting willingness to pay to reflect perceived congestion, while the second excludes those encounters which occurred on segments designated as the periphery of the area. Primarily trail segments adjoining the trail heads, these trails are summarized in appendix 4.A.

Several overall observations should be made concerning the estimates in table 6.4. First, they are quite low and are most certainly underestimates of the true aggregate willingness to pay. There are several reasons for this.

First, and of considerable significance is the fact that nothing in the survey instrument conveyed any impression that wilderness areas that could serve as alternatives to the Spanish Peaks Wilderness Area would not continue to be available to users at no charge. Accordingly, with presumed free entry to alternative close substitutes, the differences between the amounts users indicated they were willing to pay for the wilderness experiences associated with differences in the degree of congestion are much more significant than the actual amounts reflected in the responses.

In addition, it should be noted that Cicchetti and Smith were skeptical of their estimated willingness-to-pay functions as predictors of total willingness to pay. The low explanatory power of the estimated relationships when heteroscedasticity was not accounted for, as well as the factors which could not be taken into account, led them to suggest that the most important aspect of their research was the statistically significant measured effect of congestion. In any case, we noted earlier that such estimates will allow for the definition of an optimal use intensity if the true willingness to pay is a scalar function of the true value.

A second aspect of the estimates in table 6.4 which should be noted is the effect of the omission of encounters which occurred on the periphery segments. Exclusion of these encounters from the total in calculating the aggregate willingness to pay has the anticipated effect, with the estimates in the third column of the table exceeding those in the second. However, the magnitude of the effect is not as large as we might have suspected, given the number of encounters which do occur on these peripheral segments.

If we are willing to ignore the potential effects of increasing use levels on managerial and administrative costs, for the purposes of illustration, then these findings would suggest that it is not possible, based on our experiments, to define the optimal use. We do know that it exceeds 300 parties in a four-week period. The range of variation in the level of aggregate willingness to pay with respect to changes in the use intensity is not enough to accurately define the optimal use level. It appears that over the use intensities examined, the aggregate amount that users are willing to pay is increasing at a decreasing rate. However, it should be noted that the encounter measures which result from each level of use in the table are random variables. Accordingly, it is reasonable to expect some variation about the aggregate willingness-to-pay surface as we increase the total level of use. For example, the increment to aggregate willingness to pay when use increases from 240 to 270 is $257, while that observed with the increase from 270 to 300 parties was $265. At first, this appears to interrupt the declining shape of the marginal willingness-to-pay schedule. The stochastic nature of the measure of expected encounters does not preclude such behavior and makes the search for a local optimum more difficult. The results look more consistent when we examine larger variations in use, say from 180 to 240 parties and from 240 to 300. In the first case, the increment to willingness to pay is $538, while in the second it is $522. Since we cannot be sure that this willingness-to-pay function will smoothly increase to its optimum, we cannot establish with the present information the single optimal use intensity. Our findings do, however, provide valuable information for management. They suggest that if we count all encounters equally, use intensity of the Spanish Peaks can increase by more than 25 percent over 1970 levels without exceeding the optimal carrying capacity. Equally important, if we exclude the periphery encounters, then it is *not* as clear that we have, at 300 parties, reached the point of declining marginal increments to the aggregate willingness-to-pay function. This finding suggests that the role of these periphery encounters is indeed important to the definition of carrying capacity. Consequently, more research is needed to investigate the differences in the relative disruptive effects between encounters which occur at the periphery and in the interior of an area.

Table 6.5 presents the estimated encounters per party by trip length at three use intensities when the distribution of that use is uniform over the four-week period and the seven days in each week. In general, the expected encounter levels are lower than those reported in table 6.3, since the scheduling of party arrivals is more uniform than that postulated for the base case (which underlies the results in table 6.3). With these data, it is possible to examine the implications of nonprice rationing schemes for the optimal carrying capacity. That is, if we assume that the uniform weekly and daily arrivals are the result of a management action such as advance registration and assume no appreciable attendant increase in managerial and administrative costs, then a comparison of the effects of use intensity increases without alterations in these schedules and those cases with altered schedules will provide some indication of the effects of the management practice.

We are suggesting that it may be possible to increase the effective recreation capacity of a wilderness area through management policy. Moreover, in many cases such policies need not call for augmentation of the existing area or investment in new trails or campsites. While such policies also represent means of increasing the ability of an area to provide constant-quality recreational services, they are not the only means of increasing recreation capacity. In so doing, however, we must assume that this control does not affect the user's valuation of his experience. Given the character of the recreational services we are dealing with, this assumption may seem overly restrictive. Consider the manner in which this control is exercised. Clearly, if the policy calls for routine scheduling and explicit control of a party's behavior, it is reasonable to infer that there will be considerable loss in the satisfaction derived from the experience.

On the other hand, if we envision the control as less direct and not necessarily binding, such reductions might be avoided. That is, we might consider, rather than an explicit schedule for advanced registration, that the managing authority provides the recreationist with information on the anticipated use intensity of the area at the time that he wishes to come and translates this use intensity into the expected frequency with which he will encounter other parties, but allows the user to make his own decisions. A similar strategy might be taken with parties wishing to enter at a particular trail head. Management control under these schemes serves to improve the individual recreationist's information regarding what he can expect during his wilderness outing. In any case, such policies will smooth the distribution of use over the weeks and days of the season, and once we know how great the smoothing effect will be, it is then possible to determine their "value" in terms of increments to the aggregate willingness to pay.

Table 6.6 provides the estimates of aggregate willingness to pay with and without encounters on the periphery segments for each of three use intensities. As we might have expected, the reduction in estimated encounters resulting from the smoothing of arrivals increases the aggregate willingness to pay at each use intensity. This increase is more dramatic when all encounters are considered in the calculation of aggregate willingness to pay. The figures for encounters net of those on the periphery are approximately the same as those presented with the base case distribution of use. This finding also conforms to our *a priori* expectations. A smoothing of the distribution of arrivals, all else being equal, should have its greatest effects on the encounters experienced while entering and leaving the area. As the tables in chapter 4 suggest, there is a peaking in arrivals over weekends and consequently we expect a large number of periphery encounters. Smoothing the distribution of use should tend to alleviate this problem.

The implications of this management strategy are much less apparent for encounters in the interior of the area. There may be some reduction in the number of camp encounters. However, the effect is largely related to the probability distributions for route selection and is, therefore, difficult to anticipate *a priori*.

6.4   SUMMARY

In this chapter we have outlined and illustrated a method for linking the outputs of the wilderness simulation model with Cicchetti and Smith's survey research results on the preferences of wilderness recreationists. Willingness to pay has been suggested to have considerable advantages over nonmonetary measures of preferences. It does not require interpersonal comparison of satisfaction indexes, and also provides for the solution of another problem resulting from the aggregation process, namely, the implications of trip length. Nonetheless, there are limitations associated with the willingness-to-pay measure which must be recognized. They are generally of two types. First, limitations arise from the sensitivity of the measure to income distribution. And second, in the absence of markets for wilderness experiences, we must devise means for measuring individual willingness to pay.

Consider the first of these. Benefit–cost analyses have long recognized the sensitivity of any set of market prices to the existing income distribution (see Krutilla, 1961 and Eckstein, 1961). Any judgments related to the estimated level of benefits will be sensitive to that income distribution. Consequently, efficient managerial policies must be conditioned on some assumed distribution. Since the character of that distribution has been considered a normative issue, the two issues are often considered separately. We should, however, be aware that this is an artificial dichotomy.

In the absence of markets and reliable indirect means of measuring willingness to pay, the measures must be obtained through direct questioning. While it has been suggested that there are inherent biases in willingness-to-pay estimates obtained through direct solicitation, recent experiments by Bohm (1972) indicate the results are not significantly different across relevant question formats, hence weakening the presumption of bias. Moreover, this approach appears to be the only viable strategy for deriving the necessary information (i.e., willingness to pay) for the prerequisite range of wilderness experiences. Cicchetti and Smith's (1976) survey research results suggest that one can successfully measure nontime-related congestion effects with direct solicitation techniques. As we noted at the outset of this study, intrusion upon solitude as measured by encounters appears to have an important effect on individual willingness to pay.

The estimates derived by Cicchetti and Smith relate to the Spanish Peaks Area and can, therefore, be used with the outputs of our simulation model to evaluate the aggregate willingness to pay associated with each of the scenarios we discussed in this study. Our findings from a simplified coupling of these two research efforts suggest that the optimal use intensity level of Spanish Peaks, with present trail facilities and management policies, has not been reached and that use can be increased 25 percent over 1970 levels without attaining the optimal capacity. Our examination of periphery encounters versus the total encounters suggests that the effects of these encounters on individual willingness to pay is an important question with significant implications for the optimal use intensity of the area. Finally, the smoothing of arrivals has been shown to be one means of increasing the carrying capacity of the area.

REFERENCES

Becker, Gary S. 1965. "A Theory of the Allocation of Time," *The Economic Journal,* vol. 75, pp. 493–517 (September).

Bohm, Peter. 1972. "Estimating the Demand for Public Goods: An Experiment," *European Economic Review,* vol. 3 (June).

Brown, Gardner M., Jr. 1971. "Pricing Seasonal Recreation Services," *Western Economic Journal,* vol. 9 (June).

Cicchetti, C. J. 1972. "A Multivariate Statistical Analysis of Wilderness Users," in *Natural Environments: Studies in Theoretical and Applied Analysis*, edited by J. V. Krutilla (Baltimore: Johns Hopkins University Press).

————, A. C. Fisher, and V. K. Smith. 1973. "Economic Models and Planning Outdoor Recreation," *Operations Research* (September/October).

————, and V. K. Smith. 1973. "Congestion, Quality Deterioration and Optimal Use: Wilderness Recreation in the Spanish Peaks Primitive Area," *Social Science Research*, vol. 2 (March).

————, and ————. 1976. *An Econometric Analysis of Congestion Costs: The Case of Wilderness Recreation* (Cambridge, Mass.: Ballinger Publishing Co.) (forthcoming)

Clawson, Marion and J. L. Knetsch. 1966. *Economics of Outdoor Recreation* (Baltimore: Johns Hopkins University Press for Resources for the Future).

Eckstein, Otto. 1961. "A Survey of the Theory of Public Expenditure Criteria," *Public Finances: Needs, Sources and Utilization* (Princeton: Princeton University Press).

Knetsch, J. L. 1974. *Outdoor Recreation and Water Resources Planning*, Water Resources Monograph No. 3 (Washington, D.C.: American Geophysical Union).

Krutilla, J. V. 1961. "Welfare Aspects of Benefit Cost Analyses," *Journal of Political Economy*, vol. 69 (June).

Lancaster, K. J. 1966. "A New Approach to Consumer Theory," *Journal of Political Economy*, vol. 74, no. 2 (April).

Oakland, William. 1972. "Congestion, Public Goods and Welfare," *Journal of Public Economics*, vol. 1, pp. 339–357 (November).

Samuelson, P. A. 1954. "The Pure Theory of Public Expenditures," *Review of Economics and Statistics*, vol. 36, no. 4 (November).

Smith, V. K. 1975a. "Travel Cost Demand Models for Wilderness Recreation: A Problem of Non-Nested Hypotheses," *Land Economics* (May).

————. 1975b. "The Estimation and Use of Models of the Demand for Outdoor Recreation," paper prepared for National Academy of Sciences, in *Assessing the Demand for Outdoor Recreation* (Washington, D.C.: National Academy of Sciences).

Stankey, G. H. 1972. "A Strategy for the Definition and Management of Wilderness Quality," in *Natural Environments: Studies in Theoretical and Applied Analysis*, edited by J. V. Krutilla (Baltimore: Johns Hopkins University Press for Resources for the Future).

TABLE 6.1.   Estimates of Individual Willingness to Pay —
Encounters with Hiking Parties

Variable	Ordinary Least Squares[a]	Generalized Least Squares[b]
(1) Length of trip (in days)	.934 (3.887)	.780 (8.750)
(2) Length squared	-.099 (-2.763)	-.069 (-5.217)
(3) Number of encounters on the trail per day	-.114 (-2.249)	-.083 (-4.601)
(4) Number of nights of camp encounters	-.211 (-.4.011)	-.152 (-8.044)
(5) Household income (in thousands of dollars)	.013 (1.513)	.020 (6.189)
(6) Weeks of paid vacation	.045 (2.987)	.057 (8.308)
(7) Sex	.307 (2.513)	.362 (8.258)
Intercept	-.214 (-0.524)	-.354 (-2.322)
$\bar{R}^2$	.056	.756

Note: These findings are extracted from Tables 4.5 and 4.7 in Chapter 4 of the Cicchetti-Smith (1976) study.

[a] The numbers in parentheses are estimated t-ratios for the null hypothesis of no association (i.e. Ho: $\alpha_i = 0$).

[b] The $\bar{R}^2$ reported for the GLS estimates is not directly comparable to that for OLS. For a discussion of the reasons for the lack of comparability in these estimated coefficients of determination see Cicchetti and Smith (1976) Appendix to Chapter 4.

**TABLE 6.2.   Estimates of Individual Willingness to Pay —
Encounters with Riding Parties**

Variable	Ordinary Least Squares [a]	Generalized Least Squares [b]
(1) Length of trip (in days)	.671 (2.367)	.672 (6.798)
(2) Length squared	-.063 (-1.500)	-.056 (-3.870)
(3) Number of trail encounters per day	-.207 (-3.466)	-.141 (-7.526)
(4) Number of nights of camp encounters	-.288 (-4.636)	-.205 (-10.096)
(5) Weeks of paid vacation	.045 (2.549)	.056 (8.604)
(6) Sex	.285 (1.973)	.260 (5.616)
Intercept	.219 (0.480)	-.045 (-0.277)
$\bar{R}^2$	.046	.721

Note: These findings are extracted from Tables 4.6 and 4.7 in Chapter 4 of the Cicchetti-Smith (1976) study.

[a] The numbers in parentheses are estimated t-statistics for the null hypothesis of no association (i.e. Ho: α_i = 0).

[b] The $\bar{R}^2$ reported for the GLS estimates is not directly comparable to that for OLS. For a discussion of the reasons for the lack of comparability in these estimated coefficients of determination see Cicchetti and Smith (1976) Appendix to Chapter 4.

TABLE 6.3. **Estimated Expected Encounters by Trip Length and Use Intensity**

Trip Length (days)	Use Intensity[a]														
	180 Encounters			210 Encounters			240 Encounters			270 Encounters			300 Encounters		
	T-H	T-R	C	T-H	T-R	C	T-H	T-R	C	T-H	T-R	C	T-H	T-R	C
1	1.83	0.24	0.0	2.36	0.29	0.0	2.61	0.31	0.0	2.97	0.43	0.0	2.86	0.48	0.0
2	1.10	0.40	0.31	1.40	0.55	0.27	1.77	0.52	0.36	1.80	0.59	0.40	1.79	0.72	0.36
3	1.17	0.60	0.86	1.67	0.70	0.75	1.61	0.73	0.90	1.76	0.80	0.84	1.95	1.09	0.98
4	1.00	0.51	0.99	1.22	0.74	1.37	1.35	0.56	1.55	1.47	0.75	1.46	1.75	0.98	1.55
5	0.95	0.75	1.85	1.48	0.96	1.39	1.46	0.68	1.24	1.93	0.85	1.66	2.33	1.03	1.87
6	2.94	0.13	3.19	1.80	0.00	1.10	2.43	0.21	1.71	3.06	0.63	2.25	4.15	0.31	2.38
7	2.73	0.36	2.27	1.38	1.13	1.69	2.39	1.00	2.08	1.86	0.76	1.57	2.42	0.92	2.58

[a]The Use Intensity is defined in terms of the total number of parties entering the Spanish Peaks Wilderness Area in a four-week period. The encounter abbreviations are defined as: T-H = trail encounters with hiking parties, T-R = trail encounters with riding parties, C = nights with at least one camp encounter.

Structure and Properties of a Wilderness Travel Simulator

TABLE 6.4. Estimated Aggregate Willingness to Pay for Wilderness Recreation

Total Use Intensity (Parties)	Using Total Encounters in Area	Using Encounters Net of Periphery
180	$2045.	$2287.
210	$2315.	$2667.
240	$2583.	$3012.
270	$2840.	$3368.
300	$3105.	$3741.

Note: These calculations are for parties entering in a four-week period and assume that there are three individuals in each party. See note 6 for discussion of the potential bias in the estimated willingness to pay resulting from converting the dependent variable to dollar terms.

TABLE 6.5. Estimated Expected Encounters by Trip Length and Use Intensity — Uniform Weekly and Daily Use Distributions

| Trip Length (days) | Use Intensity[a] | | | | | | | | |
| | 180 Encounters | | | 240 Encounters | | | 300 Encounters | | |
	T-H	T-R	C	T-H	T-R	C	T-H	T-R	C
1	1.37	0.16	0.0	1.55	0.26	0.0	2.05	0.36	0.0
2	0.85	0.26	0.16	1.04	0.41	0.32	1.55	0.55	0.35
3	1.03	0.46	0.64	1.13	0.66	0.60	1.59	0.87	0.84
4	0.75	0.43	1.25	1.26	0.48	1.28	1.58	0.65	1.25
5	0.56	0.52	0.80	1.44	0.67	1.70	1.86	0.83	1.63
6	1.67	0.50	1.42	1.80	0.07	1.47	2.50	0.44	2.13
7	1.00	0.73	2.07	1.65	0.82	1.76	2.73	0.73	1.87

[a]The Use Intensity is defined in terms of the total number of parties entering the Spanish Peaks Wilderness Area in a four-week period. The encounter abbreviations are defined as: T-H = trail encounters with hiking parties, T-R = trail encounters with riding parties, C = nights with at least one camp encounter.

**TABLE 6.6. Estimated Aggregate Willingness to Pay for Wilderness Recreation —
Uniform Weekly and Daily Arrivals**

Total Use Intensity (Parties)	Using Total Encounters in Area	Using Encounters Net of Periphery
180	$2197.	$2278.
240	$2846.	$3141.
300	$3404.	$3895.

Note: These calculations are for parties entering in a four-week period and
assume that there are three individuals in each party. See note 6
for discussion of the potential bias in the estimated willingness to
pay resulting from converting the dependent variable to dollar terms.

CHAPTER 7

CONCLUDING REMARKS AND RESEARCH AGENDA

7.1 SUMMARY

The objective of this research has been to develop a simulation model that will mimic the travel behavior of wilderness users under varying circumstances. This information is necessary, in combination with knowledge of users' aversion to encountering other parties in the wilderness, in order to establish the optimal capacity of a wilderness area for recreation purposes. Our model is intended for managers of wilderness areas that are being subjected to mounting intensity of use. An evaluation of the effects of proposed management policies or practices can be conducted by simulated experiments, as it were, before the changes proposed are adopted.

In chapter 1 we distinguished between the economist's concept of optimal capacity and the ecologist's concept of carrying capacity. We observed that a wilderness area could provide services of varying quality given users' preferences for freedom from encountering other parties on a wilderness outing and the tendency for the frequency of encounters to increase as the intensity with which an area is used increases. In this framework, a change in the pattern of use, either through an alteration in the intensity of use or changes in its configuration over time and/or space, results in changes in the quality of the service available to users and in the amounts that they would be willing to pay for it. Our simulation model is designed to mimic such patterns of use, so that alterations in patterns or intensities of use for any particular area can be postulated, run through, and then analyzed as part of the management decision exercise.

From Stankey's research (1972) we know that persons having different preferences may use the wilderness, but management will be governed by the preferences of those whose values conform to the values reflected in the Wilderness Act and its legislative history. Solitude and freedom from intrusions upon privacy by individuals other than members of one's own party are preferred by such wilderness users. Since increasing encounters are attended by diminishing marginal benefits from any given outing for such users, the optimal level of use will obtain when the increment in the aggregate willingness to pay for wilderness recreation that results from the addition of one more user in a predetermined area and time period is just offset by the reduction in the value or benefit of the outings for all other users whom he encounters.

In order that we can determine when this point is reached, we need to be able to estimate (1) the effect of alternative levels and patterns of use on the expected frequency of encounters among parties, and (2) the effect on individual willingness to pay, or benefit, of such intrusions upon solitude and privacy. We have addressed the first of these problems in this monograph, while the second has been addressed in the study by Cicchetti and Smith (1976).

In this study we have: (1) described the simulation model developed to perform the necessary operations to obtain the estimated frequency of encounters under the various relevant circumstances, (2) studied its properties when associated with several parameterizations of our prototype wilderness area, the Spanish Peaks, and (3) outlined one simple means of using the simulation model results with the estimates of willingness-to-pay functions resulting from the Cicchetti–Smith research.

Chapter 2 outlined the basic structure of our travel simulation model. Essentially we developed an intricate scheduling model and examined the interaction between parties as they complete their own schedules. The interactions which command our primary attention are meetings or encounters on the trail and in camp. We distinguish whether they occur near the trail heads, designated as the periphery of the area, or in the interior. Encounters serve as the operational proxy for instrusions upon privacy and solitude, as suggested by Stankey's research (1972) and supported by the empirical research of Cicchetti and Smith (1973). We defined four basic components or logical parts of the model. They can be distinguished according to their respective functions as: (1) scheduling parties; (2) characterizing parties; (3) routing parties; and (4) recording each party's encounter experience.

The scheduling component distributes a fixed number of parties across the weeks of a defined season, the days of each week, and the hours of each day. Given this information, we characterize parties according to their size and mode of travel. Both of these factors can affect how they move through the area under study. For example, party size and mode of travel will generally affect the speed of movement along the trail segments of an area. The travel mode can also affect the route selected by the party for its wilderness trip. Our model simplifies the process by defining a finite number of routes which are based on actual experience. Each route specifies the exact pattern of movement of the party that selects it, including which trails are traversed and which campsites are utilized. They are assigned in the model in a probabilistic fashion with the model user's option of conditioning the process on certain key factors thought *a priori* to be important to wilderness recreationists' behavior patterns. These include the mode of travel of the party, the party's time of arrival, i.e., morning or afternoon, and the week of the season in which the party arrives. The model allows the analyst to specify a different probability distribution to determine the likelihood of any given route being selected for each combination of these factors.

Once the schedule is complete, the model executes the schedule using an event-driven clock and records each party's experiences (i.e., trail and camp encounters) while progressing through the route plan assigned to it. We should note that it is not our intention to suggest that a given party will behave this way. Rather, we suggest that our model reflects the general pattern of travel behavior when viewed in the aggregate, at the area level. It is not a behavioral model of individual actions.

The model's value as a tool for analyzing economic and management problems associated with wilderness areas is directly related to how accurately it represents the "real-world" process of low-density recreation in a given area. We addressed this issue indirectly by applying the model to a particular area. That is, we parameterized the model to conform with the physical and use characteristics of the Spanish Peaks Wilderness in Montana for the 1970 recreational season. Many compromises were necessary because of inadequate data. The simplifying assumptions underlying these compromises have been detailed in chapters 3 and 4.

Direct comparison of the simulated with the actual process is difficult and costly. One can envisage the magnitude and complexity of the task of trying to conduct controlled experiments and record outcomes when we are dealing with human beings, tens of thousands of acres of wilderness, and no effective monitoring system. Moreover, the very prospect of such an exercise and the conditions it would require is likely to be quite offensive to most of the users themselves. Fortunately, there are several alternative somewhat more approximate techniques. Solicitation of required data from users, with a user trip diary system, is one possibility. This approach provides information on one set of conditions (those in existence at the time of the diary survey). However, it does not permit the consideration of a full range of possibilities even for a single area. Nonetheless, checking the extent to which there is a correspondence between the average observed outcomes, i.e., those tabulated from user diaries, and the simulated outcomes, i.e., those tabulated within the model as parameterized to conform to the conditions existing in the area when the user diaries were surveyed, provides a rough measure of the validity of the model.

Unfortunately, data of this sort were not available and we were forced to select an approach which, in many respects, is even more rough and ready. That is, we define a base case for the area under study, the 1970 summer recreational season in the Spanish Peaks Wilderness Area, and present the results so that those familiar with the average experience in the area during this season can "judge for themselves." Clearly, this is not a completely satisfactory approach. Rather it should be viewed as a starting point for the validation of the model.

Chapter 4 outlined this base case and considered the effect of the stochastic character of the model on the sample size needed to estimate the expected experience for a given experiment with the model. Following these results, we conducted a series of sensitivity experiments with the model in order to determine if alterations in specific parameters, such as the total level of use in a season, affected encounters. We found that the total use level and its distribution over the weeks of the season and days of the week did "matter." That is, changes in these factors increased the measured encounters of certain types in the course of the simulation.

Chapter 6 proposed one simple means of using the results of the Cicchetti–Smith Spanish Peaks survey research with our simulation model. We assumed all individuals were similar in their socioeconomic characteristics, thus simplifying the aggregation process. Aggregating the encounter measures to conform with those indexes used in the Cicchetti–Smith willingness-to-pay functions, we found that use can increase by more than 25 percent over 1970 levels without reaching the optimal level. Further experimentation will be necessary to determine the optimal level of use. Nonetheless, our findings suggest that smoothing the distribution of arrivals can serve to increase the carrying capacity of the area. Moreover, the treatment of encounters near the trail head is quite important to the evaluation of the optimal level of use. There is, as all of this suggests, a great deal more work to be done. However, we feel the simulation model provides the tool necessary to assist in this research.

In what follows we will discuss the model as a managerial tool and the need for further research along two different fronts. The first concerns the application of the model to new areas and the development of an information base on its characteristics under a wide variety of alternative conditions. The second area for research, though not entirely independent of the first, can be treated separately. It concerns directions for extension and further refinement in the model itself.

7.2   THE WILDERNESS SIMULATOR
AND MANAGEMENT

A substantial amount of resources, both in manpower and computer time, have been devoted to the development of this travel simulation model. Before discussing avenues for future research with it, there should be some assessment of its potential use for current managerial problems. This is probably better performed by a task force comprised of select wilderness management personnel supported by research staff familiar with the simulator, in actual field test and demonstration applications. However, we shall attempt to discuss the potential advantages and costs of model use in objective terms.

The model is a general-purpose algorithm which can, with the appropriate data, be utilized for any recreational area. However, the postulated behavior patterns of the real-world users of these areas must conform to those assumed by the model if its outputs are to have any meaning. The data requirements of the model are not inconsequential, as chapters 2 and 3 indicated. Thus the first components of the costs of model use are associated with compiling the information necessary to parameterize the model. It is reasonable to assume that these data will not be available in precisely the form required by the model and some transformation to the required format will be necessary. As chapter 3 indicated, this information for our Spanish Peaks example was taken from available sources and supplemented by field research of one of the authors. It is probably fair to assume that some field research will also be necessary for any application. A smaller scale study by Smith and Headley (1975), of a small section of the West Canada Lakes Wilderness Area in the Adirondacks Forest Preserve, also required field research. Available maps and documentation are unlikely to be sufficient to parameterize the model accurately.

It should be noted that these costs are greatest for the initial uses. Once the data are available on the trail system and campsites, it need not be recollected for each application. It can be periodically updated to reflect any changes in the area. The information on user behavior patterns, including the arrival pattern on route assignment functions of the model, is likely to require more careful scrutiny. These relationships may be subject to more frequent change. It is difficult to assess what is involved without more experience with the information itself for each area. Despite these uncertainties, it is certainly fair to conclude that the "start-up" data costs with the model are substantial, but once the parameterization is completed, the basic data are available for innumerable applications for a long time; thus the *data costs* can be considered rather small if amortized over a substantial period that allows numerous applications.

The second major component of the costs of running the model is the computer time. The size of the area being modeled, including the trail system and campsites, as well as the number of parties using it and the duration of the season are important influences on these costs. For the Spanish Peaks model parameterized to the base case, we found the running costs close to $100 per simulation on an IBM 370-155. Using the multiple replication feature of GPSS-V allowed these costs to be reduced substantially by running the replications of a given experiment and those of different experiments at the same time (i.e., in a single processing). Average costs per replication were greatly reduced. However, our limited experience with this feature of GPSS makes summary statements hazardous, for they are likely to be sensitive to the character of the problems involved.

For smaller systems with fewer routes, trail segments, and campsites, there are rather dramatic economies in running time. Ten replications of the West Canada Lakes application with only fourteen trail segments, a smaller number of campsites, and sixteen routes cost only $30 on an IBM 370-158.[1] The number of parties involved was 100 and the season was four weeks.

Thus the model can be quite economical for small areas with limited simulation periods. It should be noted that these costs do not include the costs of summarizing the outputs of the model in conventional statistical terms. As we shall discuss in the next section, the model in its present form requires the user to perform these calculations.

What are the benefits from model use? This study has served to illustrate that the model is a rather flexible tool and allows the manager to consider alterations in management policy and practices and their implications for the quality of the "average" user's experience. The only limitations here are of ingenuity and imagination. That is, we are required to convert the policy into its effects on user arrival patterns or use patterns within the area. Once this is done, the model will translate these patterns into their implications for the quality of the users' experiences.

A wide range of managerial problems may be reviewed with little difficulty, given that the area has been modeled. Alternative investment policies in new trail systems, campsites, or other changes to given areas can be studied before they are undertaken. The value of the simulator's outputs is, of course, related to the cost of mistakes. At the margin we would like to know if the model provides enough valuable information to justify the costs involved in its use. Once a given area has been parameterized for the model, these marginal costs are likely to be quite small. Since the model was designed and constructed in response to the paucity of information on the character of wilderness experiences, it is probably fair to conclude that the information currently available for making resource allocation and managerial decisions is limited. Hence the gains may be substantial. This conclusion is especially true since we need not assume that each manager must learn to use the model himself. Rather, we might only expect familiarity with the outputs and knowledge of how to ask the questions. The task of actually running the model can be delegated to a small group or task force capable of servicing the needs of a given land management agency. An analogy may be useful here. In order to make use of the outputs of a regression program, one need not completely understand how the pro-

---

[1] It should be noted that these costs are calculated from rate schedules from university computer centers—George Washington University and the State University of New York at Binghamton. They may or may not understate the costs land management agencies will encounter in running the model.

gram actually performs the calculation. Knowledge of the correct interpretations of the output and how to assess it is all that is necessary. The same observation is true for the simulation model.

Since the cost and the utility of the model is dependent on many factors, we can only speculate as to the ultimate cost effectiveness of the methodology for wilderness and backcountry management. As not entirely unbiased observers, we are optimistic. A large measure of the uncertainty in this respect, however, will be resolved by independent evaluation following the large-scale field test–demonstration effort being currently conducted on the Desolation Wilderness of California as a cooperative Resources for the Future and Forest Service project involving both research and management personnel. More experience with actual application is required to increase the versatility and improve the efficiency of the model on the one hand, and to provide experience that will allow better evaluation of its cost effectiveness, on the other.

Before proceeding to the research agenda, we should be clear that the model does *not* require the use of willingness-to-pay functions or the framework outlined in chapter 1. The consideration of optimal management of wilderness resources motivated the decision to develop the simulation model (Fisher and Krutilla, 1972). This monograph does not seek to determine the optimal level of use of the Spanish Peaks Area. Rather, we illustrate the use of the simulator as a tool that would be necessary to such a determination.

7.3   FURTHER RESEARCH

Model Application

The performance pattern of any simulation model is related to the specific parameterizations of the model that are investigated. Simply stated, the frame of reference affects the evaluation of policy options. Accordingly, it is desirable to know first hand just how sensitive the values of the various outputs of the model are to alterations in the parameter values. When the model is as complex as our travel simulator, the range of values for each parameter (or probability distribution) and the alternative configurations of values for all parameters increases the sample space of potential parameterizations of the model to unmanageable proportions. That is, we can define so many different parameterizations of the model that it appears that a complete sensitivity analysis of the model as a logical process would be impossible.

Fortunately we have the ability to reduce this sample space of potential parameterizations of the simulator. We are concerned with the model's performance in those cases in which it is likely to be used, i.e., for existing low-density recreational areas (both *de facto* and *de jure* wilderness areas).[2] Accordingly, the sample space is reduced from all conceivable configurations to those based on real-world areas. While this introduction of additional information to constrain the choices for alternative specifications of the model is important and reduces the sensitivity problem to manageable proportions, it nonetheless indicates that additional work on the model may be fruitful.

For example, we examined the effects of transit-time variability (i.e., 5, 12, and 20 percent coefficients of variation). Our findings suggest that encounters were not appreciably affected under the base case scenario for the Spanish Peaks area. We cannot immediately conclude that this result is readily applicable to all wilderness areas and levels of use. It relates to the Spanish Peaks area for levels of use in a reasonable neighborhood of the base case level. Does this caution mean that we must re-address every issue with every area? We think not.

What it does imply is that we need to gain experience with the model with a set of different areas and attempt to define the "extreme" cases, i.e., those model parameterizations which are most different. If we find that a specific parameter's value is not particularly important to the measured outputs of the model in these extreme cases, then it is probably safe to conclude that the model is rather insensitive to it for practical purposes. Accordingly, it would seem that the application of the simulator to a variety of areas with different physical characteristics and use patterns could serve an important research purpose as well as aid in obtaining information of direct utility to those concerned with practical management problems.

Our strategy in testing the model, as we have noted, should be viewed as a first step. The resources, both informational and other, were not adequate for the kind of full-scale sensitivity study which we have discussed. Such a study would include consideration of alternative probability distributions for routes, which would be defined in terms of that set of specifications that are thought to be possible for the Spanish Peaks Wilderness Area. We cannot consider our study of use levels as definitive. Larger total use intensities as well as alternative (reasonable) configurations of hourly, daily, and weekly patterns should be examined. The investigation we have conducted of the implications of within-party-type variability in transit time does not help us to evaluate the implications of alternative assumptions regarding the variability in transit times among parties of different sizes and modes of travel. Since the values we used in the latter cases were regarded as the best "guessestimates," further attention may well be warranted here.

The routes themselves were based on a sample of users' reports for the summer of 1970. We should study the extent to which these are repre-

---

[2] This point has also been made with respect to statistical estimators and holds generally for all tools of analysis (see Smith 1972).

sentative of today's pattern of use, and if they are not, to what extent any differences in the routes affect the model's outputs.

Once some of these basic issues are more fully answered, we can begin to address the possibility of summarizing the behavior of the model with response surface techniques. That is, we design a set of experiments for the model parameterized to conform to a given area to estimate with multivariate statistical techniques the relationships between our output measures, i.e., trail and camp encounters, and the factors of interest for the area in question.

The simulation model describes a complex probabilistic process in which a number of variables such as use intensity, party-type mix, arrival patterns, and route probability functions determine the measured encounters for each party using the area. Response surface techniques attempt to approximate this process with specific functional relations between measures of the inputs to and the outputs of the model.[3] Accordingly, they can be particularly useful for gauging the approximate effect of certain variables. For example, suppose that we estimated with ordinary least-squares regression techniques an equation for each encounter measure aggregated by trip length as a function (say a polynomial approximation) of the total level of use. If these estimated relationships evidenced a reasonably good fit, then we might interpret the estimated coefficients as providing an indication of the marginal effect on encounters of increased use.

Estimates of these relations would allow the manager to narrow the range of experiments over which he would need to perform simulations in evaluating policy alternatives. Equally important, they would provide an alternative means of determining economic carrying capacity if they are used in conjunction with the estimated aggregate willingness-to-pay functions to solve analytically for the optimum level of use. Clearly, the solution would be an approximate one. However, it could be further checked with additional simulations employing use intensities in the neighborhood of the estimated optimum.

In further applications of the model, we can envisage that a number of alternative strategies for use may develop, and these strategies will need to be evaluated. For example, the modeling of large-scale systems beyond the capacity (core storage) of the program, in terms of the number of trail segments and campsites, may require partitioning the system into subareas and treating each as a separate system. The connecting trails between subareas can be treated as exit points for one area and trail heads for the other. Routes will need to be defined in terms of the partitioned system, as will the probability distributions. However, it would seem that we can, in principle, accommodate any area with such an approach. We

[3] Some discussion of these issues, as well as an extensive bibliography of the literature on response surface techniques, is found in Burdick and Naylor (1969).

do lose the ability to track individual parties and maintain unique records on them to the extent they move between subareas. It should be noted, however, that translating the "principles" to practice is often most difficult and that only by attempting to apply the model to larger systems will we develop a full understanding of the possible complexities involved.[4]

Our work with the Spanish Peaks application focused on a four-week period early in the recreation season. It will also be necessary to simulate subsets that occur in the middle of the season. At the outset of the simulation under these circumstances, there will likely be parties within the area. All the routes defined in our examples begin at trail heads and the model is initialized without any parties in the area. Simulation of periods in the middle of the recreational season will require the definition of routes that originate in the interior of the area. They are hypothetical routes in that they are simply a means of placing parties in the interior segments of the area to conform to a distribution within an area that has been in use. Precisely how these are designated and how we count the encounter records of these parties in our aggregate tables are questions which still need to be addressed.

The preceding discussion is by no means exhaustive. It serves only to illustrate that much work is yet to be done in order to more fully understand the model and the problems associated with its application to complex real-world wilderness recreational patterns.

Model Development

As noted previously, the travel simulation model discussed throughout this volume was developed to serve two objectives: (1) To provide one means of assessing the effects of alternative use patterns and management policies on the experiences of recreationists in a given area without the need to actually observe them for each case in the real world. (2) To describe in economic terms the equivalent of the production process for wilderness recreation, with explicit attention given to quality. These are not incompatible aims and we feel that the present model serves both reasonably well. This should not, however, imply that there is no scope for improvement.

There are a variety of problems quite similar in character to the ones advantageously represented with our model, which cannot be accommodated by the model in its present form. One example of a class of applications is wilderness recreation at the Boundary Waters Canoe Area. In this

---

[4] It should be noted that this deficiency is being corrected through further development of the model in a more demanding application of the simulator to the heavily used Desolation Wilderness Area. This work is being carried out by Mordechai Shechter at RFF in cooperation with Robert Lucas of the U.S. Forest Service.

case the activity is primarily water-based canoe trips. Accordingly, in the terminology of our model, the trails are not well defined. Equally, if not more important, the character of the party-to-party interaction is somewhat different from that of trail encounters in land-based low-density recreation. Campsites will be along the waterways and therefore allow for considerable trail-to-camp interaction. Encounters of this type are not considered in the present version of the model. It is reasonable to expect that such encounters do represent disruptions of solitude and consequently must be taken into account. It has also been suggested that the trail-to-camp encounter is an important omission from the model for land-based recreational activities. In principle, the logic of the program can be amended to include them.

Another important extension of the model concerns the addition of program logic which would allow the user to obtain summary statistics for multiple replications of a single experiment. At present the model can be run for independent replications of a given experiment using GPSS V's CLEAR option. However, it does not have the capability necessary to calculate the summary statistics and analysis-of-variance tests we have performed. Using the GPSS HELP block approach, a user can code the equivalent of subroutines to perform these calculations. Accordingly, it is possible and desirable to add these capabilities to the model.

It will be necessary also to consider measures of what we will call the "within-group" variation in experiences. Throughout our analysis we have assumed the analyst is interested in the average experience. We do not have a measure of the variation about this average. That is, while we have the variation in the average experience across independent replications of a given experiment, we do not have measures of the variation across individual parties in a single replication. There is a need to utilize summary statistics, since we will need to treat them as random variables and average their values over the independent replications of each experiment.

All of this discussion should illustrate that we consider the model a developing tool and hope that some experience will be gained with it in its present form before extensive modifications are undertaken. There are a number of refinements that can and should be made. However, the model in its present form can be a useful tool not only in managerial problems but also in answering questions concerning how important it is to obtain data of various sorts. For example, we found that the treatment of encounters occurring on the periphery has important implications for the definition of economic carrying capacity. In chapter 6 we made some rather arbitrary assumptions for their relative effects on willingness to pay. Our simulation model indicated that they are not an inconsequential component of the total and accordingly behavioral research should be directed to the study of the differences between individual recreationists' reactions to encounters on the periphery as compared with the interior of a wilderness area.

Similarly, the model can eliminate the need for data collection. Our preliminary testing of the sensitivity of our encounter estimates to within-group variability in transit time indicated that further work to refine these data may not be warranted. It may be that after further testing with the model parameterized for other areas, our tentative judgment in this respect will be confirmed.

In concluding, it should be emphasized that this model does not make decisions on managerial policy or resource allocation. It provides the information useful for efficient decision making. Ultimately the decisions must be based on some objective function. Whether the management authority's, or a measure of willingness to pay, it is the objective function that values the outcomes the model provides. As economists we are inclined toward a measure such as aggregate willingness to pay in spite of its difficulties. This preference does not prevent the model from being effectively used without the willingness-to-pay function. However, in such a case, it will require the user to supply the valuation weights.

REFERENCES

Burdick, D. S. and T. H. Naylor. 1969. "Response Surface Designs," in *The Design of Computer Simulation Experiments,* edited by T. H. Naylor (Durham, N.C.: Duke University Press).

Cicchetti, C. J. and V. K. Smith. 1973. "Congestion, Quality Deterioration and Optimal Use: Wilderness Recreation in the Spanish Peaks Primitive Area," *Social Science Research* (March).

————, and V. K. Smith. 1976. *An Econometric Analysis of Congestion Costs: The Case of Wilderness Recreation* (Cambridge, Mass.: Ballinger Publishing Co., forthcoming).

Fisher, A. C. and J. V. Krutilla. 1972. "Determination of Optimal Capacity of Resource Based Recreation Facilities" in *Natural Environments: Studies in Theoretical and Applied Analysis,* edited by J. V. Krutilla (Baltimore: Johns Hopkins University Press for Resources for the Future).

Smith, V. K. 1972. "The Small Sample Properties of Selected Econometric Estimators in the Context of Alternative Macro-Models," *International Statistical Review* (December).

Smith, V. K. and R. L. Headley. 1975. "The Use of Simulation Models in Wilderness Management: A Case Study of the Adirondack Forest Preserve," in *Management Science Applications to Leisure Time,* edited by Shaul Ladany (Amsterdam: North-Holland).

G. H. Stankey. 1972. "A Strategy for the Definition and Management of Wilderness Quality," in *Natural Environments: Studies in Theoretical and Applied Analysis,* edited by J. V. Krutilla (Baltimore: Johns Hopkins University Press for Resources for the Future).

Library of Congress Cataloging in Publication Data

Smith, Vincent Kerry, 1945–
    Structure and properties of a wilderness
travel simulator.

    1.   Wilderness areas—Recreational use—Data
processing.   2.   Wilderness areas—Visitors—Mathe-
matical models.   3.   Spanish Peaks Wilderness, Mont.
I.   Krutilla, John V., joint author.   II.   Title:
Structure and properties of a wilderness
travel simulator . . .
GV191.67.W5S64   333.7'8   75-33766
ISBN 0-8018-1808-7